DON'T CALL ME "MAESTRO"

My Manuscript is divided into two parts. The first half is written in such a way as to present all the vocal wisdom I have garnered over the years into the most expedient form possible.

The subject of each and every page is self explanatory.

A vocal survival guide for those who desperately wish to improve what they've got to work with.

The second half consists of several hundred lessons I had recorded on tape pared down to its bare essentials in order to acquaint the student as to what actually occurs during a lesson... or should have.

DON'T CALL ME MAESTRO

Text, photos, artwork, and design copyright © 1998 by Gunnar Filip Peterson

First edition published by Philomel Publishers (aka Gunnar Filip Peterson) 1998

Original typesetting and design by Kent Darling Design, Pacifica, CA

Library of Congress Control Number: 2021900082

ISBN 978-1-7363611-9-1

SECOND EDITION

DEDICATION

To those trusting and faithful students forced into remission by forces beyond their ability to control.

Victimized by the fables of a charlatan, they have fallen by the wayside, never to realize their true potential, and consequentially... harbor a "Phantom Pain" that persists for years afterward.

Contents

Section 8: Beyond the Studio - Auditions and Other Tortures   101

Section 9   113

1

The Nitty-Gritty Bedrock

caveat emptor

Preface

Modus Operandi

The Jigsaw Puzzle

Forever and a Day

An Ear Above Your Own

The Myth of "Bel Canto"

Books on "Sinking"

Excuses

A "Golden Throat"

The Awareness of Not Knowing

"Emminent Specialists"

Quantum Sufficit

Prior Convictions

Not to be Trifled With

X Marks the Spot

An Old Empirical Concept

Breathless

"Support"

VOCAL TOMBSTONES

This "Maestro" has delusions of adequacy.

He sets low vocal standards and consistently fails to achieve them.

caveat emptor

$$

The La Calunnia School of Bel Canto Concepts and Coaching

Curses in All Aspects of the Vocal Arts

Student understands that it is highly probable that errors and omissions

will occur in any vocal teaching process, especially when large numbers of singers are developed and maintained; notwithstanding, student agrees to take each lesson "as is" fully expecting that there may be errors and omissions in the data obtained from the lesson.

Student understands and agrees that Maestro makes absolutely no warranty whatsoever, whether expressed or implied, as to the accuracy thoroughness, value, quality, validity, marketability, suitability, condition or fitness for a particular purpose of the data and any programming used to obtain the data in the form desired by student, nor as to whether the data is up-to-date, complete or based upon accurate or meaningful facts.

signature_____

have a nice lesson

$$$

PREFACE

As gifted as any neophyte may believe himself to be, he approaches a teacher with only one thought in mind. He wants to sing better.

Why should any student be denied that and instead suffer the physical and psychological consequences of studying with an incompetent teacher?

Is it really so difficult to free up an instrument?

Not really.

Cannot knowledge be imparted in such a manner as to eliminate confusion and the resulting hysteria between student and teacher?

I should hope so.

Is there really so much to know and absorb?

A helluva lot more than you ever thought possible.

Usually a student garners only as much knowledge as his teacher possesses so this book proposes a common meeting ground, bridging the gap between apparently diverse, conflicting, and more often than not, dense and impenetrable viewpoints.

Because singing is based primarily upon sound identification, this book

has no voice except in the printed sense, and therefore cannot teach you to recognize good technique with your ears, but only with your mind.

Still, like every good captain of old sailing the uncharted seas, you must take advantage of any and all material that may possibly be to your advantage.

I do hope the "charts" I offer will help you plot a true course.

Modus Operandi

There are as many "Methods" of singing as there are religions. Depending upon your nature, some will work for you… and some will not.

In politics, the opposition will hang you from the yardarm.

In society, the non-smokers will nail you to the cross.

In voice training, the "beautiful tone" glorifiers will brook no deviant doctrines. "Small" voices will remain small. "Short tops" will never exceed their limitations. Big, dark voices will never achieve flexibility. Those with an inborn sensitivity to the text will never discover or develop it while diction is sacrificed to "tone."

Your "comfort zone" has always been the "beautiful tone" practitioners prime directive.

Everyone goes to hell in a basket, in their own way… name your poison!

Any self-imposed exclusion that would perhaps challenge whatever beliefs you may have acquired will always limit your chances of vocal survival.

All I have attempted to do is to SIMPLIFY… to puzzle out the truth (as I see it) in a sane and sober way, to work through the misconceptions that pervade and prostitute this truth in the name of "Bel Canto"

Nothing more. Nothing less.

Naturally (in common with the rest of humanity) I'm prejudiced in my own behalf!

The Jigsaw Puzzle

All singers attempt in their own way to assemble the intricate jigsaw puzzle (what else can you call it?) that constitutes the process of learning how their mechanism operates.

When they discover a part of the puzzle that does not seem to fit their

particular viewpoint, they discard it.

By the time they begin to understand what the picture should look like, they have discarded or thrown away half the parts.

Is it any wonder they are incomplete?

Everything must fit together.

Mother Nature demands it!

Forever and a Day

Fish gotta swim, birds gotta fly, and I was no exception.

I was stricken early with the "Sing or Die" syndrome.

Nothing else mattered. The only thing going for me was perseverance, and a very exacting voice teacher. Even though she was saddled with more than her share of "problem" students, they all prospered and improved.

I was born a tenor, although, at first, many of those hearing me sing felt I must be a baritone… with delusions of grandeur.

My larynx was far larger than that of any other singer I had ever met. I also had the ability to descend to the lower depths, much to the frustration of a basso friend of mine, who could not quite match my "tones", although both of us benefited enormously from each others' "expertise"

Absolutely refusing to become a "short" tenor, I engaged in a tug of war with my crico-thyroid muscles for almost twenty years!

These muscles (the tensors of the vocal cords) were, in me, akin to a recalcitrant clam, insisting upon clamping up, and closing down my instrument.

In my attempt to conquer the inherent balkiness in the upper part of my

non-existent tessitura, I was in essence, attempting to rebuild Mother Nature's malfunctions.

Yes, it can be done, but, I never thought it would take… Forever and a Day!

An Ear Above Your Own

Self-help books in every category propagate each other.

Perhaps one day you may even see a cat at the dinner table with a knife

and fork in each paw! Stranger things have happened.

But this much you do know; he didn't learn to do it by himself.

Vocal "Methods" are no exception. Regardless of your imagined

proficiency in any other "self-taught" subject, the need for a teacher in

singing is mandatory.

You need a discerning ear above and beyond your own.

The Myth of "Bel Canto"

The stuff and nonsense purveyed by self-styled adherents of the "bel canto tradition" prove to me only one thing: there really exists no tradition at all!

The phrase is meaningless. I'd sooner believe in the tooth fairy.

No such tradition exists outside the "ear" of the hearer and a few maxims of a general nature.

A plethora of aphorisms, like a horde of locusts, descends upon the head of the poor student, who will presumably welcome them with the fervor of a true believer.

Why not … what does he know?

Herein lies all the confusion; the "tradition" offers no hard and fast rules of technique to explain exactly how and why the voice works.

Since the day he was born, he has learned through aphorisms * A penny saved; early to bed; the other pasture; a stitch in time; etc. … So what!

Now he must contend with these "Commandments from Above":

"Hollow head, full throat, broad chest, tight waist" etc.

All well and good, but this is not going to feed a hungry stomach.

Where is there anything written I can put to a practical use?

Practically nowhere.

Books On "Sinking"

All "voice" books do serve a purpose.

Some even contain relevant information!

If the student could conceivably separate the wheat from the chaff he would no doubt profit from it.

Intuition and a gut instinct for what is workable or of a practical value, demands a common sense approach.

Forearmed in this manner, he might at least know what to expect.

However, were he to read all the voice books in existence, he would no doubt hie himself off to the nearest psychiatrist!

101 uses for a "used" vocal primer; Foot stool, roofing material, charcoal igniter, garbage liner…

Excuses

Everyone has an "operatic" voice, or at least a reasonable facsimile thereof, even though this may not be readily apparent.

Those that deny this power in themselves have plenty of excuses

"I only sing for my own amusement."

"I have no interest in opera, I would prefer to sing only in concerts and lieder recitals."

"I'm very comfortable singing in the tessitura I was born with."

"I wasn't born with a great voice and my former teacher told me I really didn't have much to work with."

"Hey, voice isn't everything! I more than make up for it with my acting, dancing, interpretation, charisma, etc. Who needs it?"

"I'm not going to spend good money on something I already know!"

A word of caution… don't lend this book out to any of the above… you'll never get it back.

The sour grape philosophers of the world have always sought to ban or burn anything contrary to their own pre-ordained prejudices.

A "Golden Throat"

How often have I heard this expression used!

Gold may be where you find it, but believe it or not, that's the easy part! There's still a long, long trail awinding.

First you have to dig it up; then you have to smelt it; then you have to refine it; then finally the day may come… when you can begin to create an object of beauty out of this material.

There are no guarantees.

But I will promise you this… no instrument, however gorgeous, can survive without proper care and training.

The impurities inherent in any instrument, unless ironed out, will eventually magnify, multiply, and corrode what had been a cherished possession.

The Awareness of Not Knowing

For over 40 years I have sought out, any which way I could, the nitty-gritty, absolutely practical, common-sense vocal principles upon which I could depend to achieve my heart's desire. My only voice teacher, Alma Michelini, started me off in the right direction.

I always assumed her practical common-sense approach was the norm... how wrong I was! Many of the principles she advocated are either basically unknown, or totally ignored. As the years began to add up, I kept asking myself... how the hell could this be?

Then one day it dawned on me... it was always this way! Always!

Hers was a voice in the wilderness.

I at least had a target to shoot for... because she taught me to understand the difference between what I did not know and what I had to know... what I was doing... and why.

In essence, you, as a student, may well be studying with some one who hasn't the foggiest notion that there does, indeed, exist a wellspring of knowledge known to a privileged few, and is therefore entirely unaware of his or her ignorance in this capacity. Now that's heartbreaking!

Gold is where you find it. And, in the same vein.. a voice teacher whose students actually do improve is worth his or her weight in gold.

"Eminent Specialists"

Rummage through some of the voice manuals, articles, essays, etc. of the distant and not so distant past and you will find some rather hilarious roads to vocal salvation.

Each and every one of these "eminent specialists" in vocal chaos was very adamant in his or her viewpoint:

Breath, breath, and more breath! At least six months of breathing lessons before commencing singing lessons!

A specialist must examine (prior to study) the nose, because a good tone is just not possible without a well-formed nose without obstructions...

If the tone is nasal, vocal exercises can scarcely be expected to remedy this obvious defect of the vocal apparatus.

Anyone beginning voice lessons after the age of thirty must realize... his or her voice is already past its prime.

Such "enlightened" pronouncements of the guardians of vocal purity have caused as much (or more) destruction as did Genghis Khan!

These miscreants are depriving villages somewhere ... of IDIOTS.

Quantum Sufficit

I know there will be a helluva lot of teachers out there who will dispute some portions of what I have written… fair enough.

I believe a good contralto to be the rarest of all voices, but this voice can be trained easily enough, especially if it is recognized and appreciated for what it is.

The one voice that usually falls by the wayside, is, of course, the tenor. A good tenor is also an endangered species… there are plenty of them out there… but very few of them can boast of an easy and agreeable high C.

So few that a tenor that has one may well feel he deserves the right to prove to one and all that he is quite capable of outshining any of his colleagues… regardless of the fact that they may be far better trained and more experienced than he is.

My teacher seemed almost to specialize in the tenor voice.

All of her students got better and better. Perhaps she may have felt that since they were the the most difficult voices to train, they posed a greater challenge… I don't know.

But this I can attest to… the proof is in the pudding!

One student she had to deal with was an asthmatic; had a New York accent you could cut with a knife; a big, raw, baritone quality, that didn't spin or turn over; a student whose tongue consistently came up with the pitch, and a voice that topped out on a G natural.

But this ain't all! He was a tenor to boot!

Teacher, put yourself to the test! If you think you know it all, and have what it takes to teach, you find a student with as little going for him as I had.

You'll find out soon enough… if you've got the "right stuff"

Prior Convictions

A Trivial Pursuit in the never ending quest for your own version of a

"Unique Technique."

How knowledgeable do you visualize yourself to be in the "Vocal Arts" field? Well, here's your chance to prove to one and all that you do, indeed, know far more than any one had ever suspected... or even gave you credit

for knowing.

Now, these are subjective images of an imaginary nature and needless to say... they will be counted against you.

"When singing high, think low... when singing low, think high."

"Float the tone on the breath like a ball on a fountain of water."

"Keep that egg shape in the back of your throat."

"Keep broadening your face till you feel your head floating."

Listed below are the five principles of an objective technical nature upon which you will defend to your dying day.. no holds barred!

1-

2-

3-

4-

5-

Anything you say, can, and will be used against you!

P.S. I would advise using a pencil. After reading this book...

you may wish to fudge a little.

X Marks the Spot

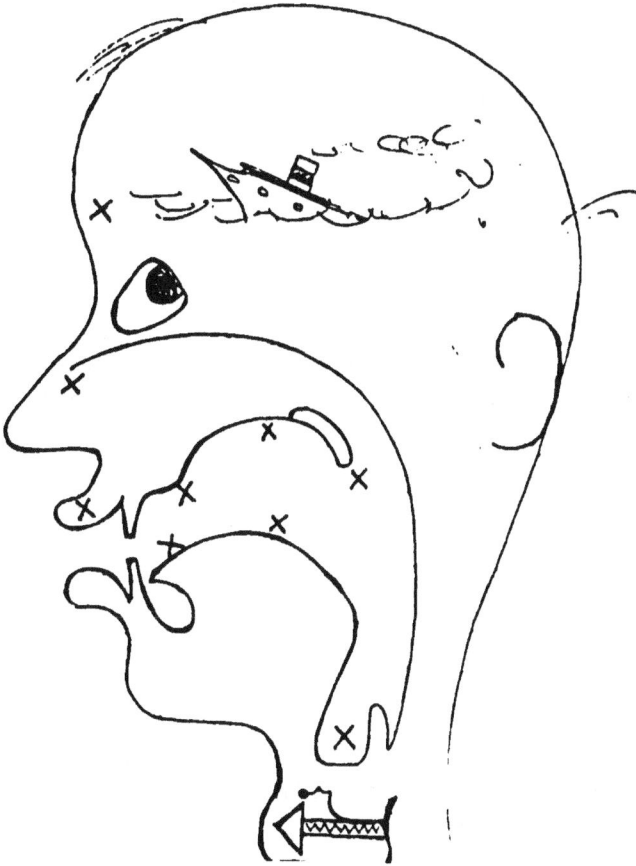

You say you have diligently studied and embraced the precepts advocated by famous singers and distinguished teachers of voice?

Well, now, you should have no trouble at all answering the following questions.

1 - The vowel in every voice is located precisely... where?

2 - The center of the focus of resonance in every voice is located precisely... where?

3 - What three consonants and only these three consonants _ _ _ _ _ _ _ have the ability to create a placement?

B C D F G H J K L M N P Q R S T V W X Y Z

An Old Empirical Concept

Student:	Wonderful. Now that you have told me what to do, please explain to me why I should do it!
Teacher:	When I tell you to push the piano with your diaphragm, that means I want you to "support"
Student:	Support what, the piano?
Teacher:	The "Tone"
Student:	The tone has to be supported?
Teacher:	Naturally.
Student:	Why?
Teacher:	Because the diaphragm supports the air, which in turn supports the tone; otherwise the tone would fall back into your throat.
Student:	But you told me the tone was produced in the throat!
Teacher:	Yes, but we have to strengthen the diaphragm that supports the air that supports the tone produced by the throat, in order to prevent the tone from falling back into the throat after we get the tone up and out of the throat!
	Now isn't that obvious?
Student:	Huh?

The next lesson the student appears upon his teacher's doorstep armed with a set of barbells.

(What does he know? He's doing the best he can!)

Breathless

Some things occur in life that one never forgets. Years later they become relevant although at the time they seemed to be of no consequence.

In the barracks I was assigned to in 1945, one member of my squad habitually talked in his sleep. It was sometimes annoying... but always good for a laugh (barracks humor).

Having no inhibitions to stifle him, he rambled on and on.

He was quite coherent, and, at times, his voice rose and fell in pitch!

Obviously, he was totally unconcerned about his breath control, diaphragmal "support" or what have you. He just rambled on!

Makes you wonder!

"Support"

This inspired bit of non compos mentis from the distant past has become the reigning password of anyone pretending to know how the voice works.

In essence it means to "shore up" or sustain.

Shore up what? Sustain what? And why?

Every teacher conjures up his own hypothesis. No two are alike.

One thing they do agree upon: the almost mystical influence of airflow necessary to sustain the "tone"... must be brought under the students' conscious control.

Give me a break!

People betting at the racetrack have been known to talk to horses ... maybe it helps ... I don't know.

The diaphragm (being a sheet of involuntary muscles) has its own set of rules and obeys its own inclinations.

You might as well try to harness your heartbeat.

When your teacher admonishes you for not "supporting" your voice, it usually means you are practicing "clavicular" breathing; that is, using the muscles around your collarbone to take in air; just filling the top portion of your lungs and not your whole system.

Therefore, you'll naturally run out of breath sooner than you should.

2

The Dynamic Duo

Breath Control?

The "Canary" Concept

"Eminence" is No Recommendation

Accentuate the Positive

Recitativo

Diction

Not to be Trifled With

Intonation

Not so Prime Directives

Pronunciation Guide

Multiple Choices

The Great "Tone God"

An Old Empirical Concept

The Dominant Vowel

Mistaken Identity

Thy Dominant Vowel

The Pure Vowel and Nothing But

Birds of a Feather

The Dynamic Duo

If mankind had no vocal cords to begin with... I would presume everyone would greet each other with grunts.

Mother Nature, in her infinite wisdom, has seen fit to provide us with more than one cord... two in fact!

This foresight on her part may have been meant only to alleviate the dreariness and the obvious monotony of conversing on a single pitch.

(hell, I don't know)

Now the primary vibrations induced by the vocal cords are almost inaudible, and only attain their full glory and splendor when the resonating cavities of the pharynx, the mouth, nose, and sinus bequeath their fair share of amplification.

Although you may subconsciously feel the rest of your body vibrating in sympathy (which is a good thing), this is more an expression of emotional well-being, than a sign of any contributions to the voice made by the liver, hip joint, knee cap, whatever.

Breath Control?

Some voice teachers have enough sense to realize that excess air can be a student's greatest threat, and therefore must be banished from the realm... by any and all presumably potent incantations known to man or beast.

Every book ever written on the subject of vocal supremacy supports the belief that the most stringent precautions must be taken at all times to control the flow of this energy.

The vocal cords are activated mentally; they will vibrate on any chosen pitch... almost but not quite independent of any air supply whatsoever.

They need some air of course, but a breeze is more to be desired than

a hurricane.

Those that advocate the breath as being the mainstay, the one predominant force, that must be harnessed before any kind of progress can be made...

are barking up the wrong tree!

As impressive as this theorem has proven to be for those who practice it...

I still maintain it is a waste of time and money.

I've said it before, and I will say it again... breathing does not develop singing... singing develops breathing.

The "Canary" Concept

Practicing one morning, endeavoring to do everything I had taught myself,

I was musing about the term "Canary" as applied to the female vocalists of a bygone age.

Could this term imply a forgotten concept? Ding, Ding, bells start to ring!

I normally imagined my larynx to be held in the palm of my hand straight out in front of me. This serves a dual purpose. It relieves most of the muscular tensions that always arise while warming up, and also reinforces the idea of going "out" for what I want.

I now visualized a canary in place of my larynx.

Naturally a canary belongs not in my hand but "in my throat."

Performing a minor "sleight of hand" I now had the canary.. firmly lodged in my throat!

I was astounded by the freedom I now possessed; all my natural tensions had vanished!

Trusting my instrument to do the right thing, I sang with a vengeance!

After a few moments however, I began to understand, that this temporary "fix" could only be carried so far, and no further.

Imagination is a wonderful attribute... it sure makes things easier!

But be forewarned...

This creative concept may indeed free up your instrument for the moment... but, it has its limits. Under no circumstances, can it be relied upon to permanently correct technical inadequacy!

"Eminence" is No Recommendation

Harken to a less than enchanted reviewer's comment concerning the lead soprano (an eminent voice teacher, no less) in a newly discovered Gilbert and Sullivan opera… "in retrospect I must mention, that until that moment, I never quite realized what a lovely language… Yiddish could be!"

Every composer chooses to set to music words that express thoughts he himself wishes to convey. (at least I should hope so!)

The emotions involved in singing are presumed to transcend those conveyed by the speaking voice. In capturing and expressing emotions with music… speech becomes song. Song is glorified speech.

In all dramatic arts involving the singing voice, but especially opera, this is what should be; but too often the words get lost in the shuffle.

To put it bluntly; "rendered" incomprehensible.

The verb oratory, has at least nine different definitions.

For your edification, I shall list them.

Articulate, enunciate, express, intonate, phrase, pronounce, speak, verbalize, and vocalize.

There, in a nutshell… is what "singing", is all about!

In other words, singing is nothing more than "Inflamed Oratory", and you damned well better believe this!

Accentuate the Positive

Brought up in New York, I shared a common affliction with the rest of the natives: the infamous accent.

Only during the course of my first few lessons did I become aware of this, and, in turn, of my teacher's passionate concern for the proper articulatory process influencing each and every word.

Since the pitch or the melodic line in any piece of music soon becomes entirely subconscious, I began to realize the importance of the words as the propelling force in any melodic message to be delivered.

Recitativo

Arias are meant to be sung and recitativo is meant to be spoken.

The mere mention of this word recitativo provokes an immediate glazing of the eyeballs.

No singer is immune.

Recitativo means exactly what it means … spoken dialogue.

You must learn to deal with it on its own terms … not yours!

Herein lies all the difficulty.

What the hell are you talking about?

Arias (for the most part) are almost always learned by rote.

While the artist in question may have a rudimentary knowledge of the language and even of the text involved, this is of secondary importance.

His only concern has always been to ride the crest of the melodic line... and make "beautiful tones"

Lohengrin's Narrative, Pari Siamo, Ella Giammai M'amo, and even the incomparable Caro Nome... all gain an extra measure of truth when "spoken" or "intoned"

Intonation is the keyword.

Recitativo, Declamato, Sprechstimme... all share the same bed.

DICTION

GOOD DICTION - consists of correct pronunciation, clear enunciation and distinct articulation.

PRONUNCIATION - the utterance of words with regard to sound and to accent.

ENUNCIATION - the manner of that utterance as regards fullness and clearness.

ARTICULATION - the action of the speech organs in the formation of consonants, vowels and syllables

The only medium for forming and sustaining vocal "tone" is the vowel.

The vowel should first be established in pure form and not changed until it is time to pronounce the next vowel or consonant.

The function of the consonant is to launch the vowel without doing violence to it.

Not to be Trifled With

Everything in the process of learning how to sing is really a trifle. Each and every trifle must be attended to. You can't neglect or slough over any of them. It's the same with your car or any other piece of machinery. Sooner or later, anything wrong with it will come back to haunt you.

How many trifles are there? Each consonant; each vowel; each word; each phrase; each and every bit of the knowledge necessary to expand the ability of your instrument to deliver.

In round numbers... at least a thousand!

Intonation

The dictionary defines intonation as (1) the use of musical tones in speaking or chanting or (2) to utter in a singing voice.

When conversing in the English language, it simply means we subconsciously stress a change in the length, the volume and especially the pitch of a word, to convey our innermost thoughts.

Interpretation (aside from the musical values) is almost entirely dependent upon the various ways we can form a thought and turn it into a sentence.

Not so Prime Directives

Beset by a host of conflicting terms and vocal absurdities in his teacher's method, each student instinctively fixates upon that one particular parcel of knowledge he deems necessary to improve his vocal progress.

Nothing wrong with this.

I've done it. Every one I've ever known has done it.

The problem lies not with the student picking out this prime directive but with the KIND of directive he inevitably picks: "place it in the mask" "put an egg in your throat""let your head float on top of your neck."

Subjective images, masquerading as objective technique.

They call not for perspiration but inspiration!

Somehow, someday, after an indefinite period of muddling through scales and the Italian Song Book, the teacher will say it for the millionth time and the student will suddenly "get it"

Voila! Instant opera star.

That being the case, why pick a more demanding directive requiring hard work and specific attention to details? Why settle for slow steady progress beginning today when you can have sudden perfect enlightenment sometime in the future?

Aye… there's the rub. Of all the mandates descending from above, the

student will almost never fix on, in fact will always short-shrift, the articulatory process.

Damn near everything wrong with any instrument that can deliver, can be traced to the singer's inability to articulate correctly!

In their quest for vocal wisdom, the great majority of students find the articulatory process to be both tedious and time-consuming.

With very few exceptions, I have never heard any singer vehemently defending the consonant as the wellspring of technique.

There's nothing "bel canto" about it. It's hard work!

Pronunciation Guide

In this book, as in the lessons I've taught, there are six basic vowel markers I've taught to convey all vowel sounds found in operatic texts. They are:

AY as in Lay

EE as in Free

IE as in Pie

OE as in Moe

AW as in Law

OO as in Who are You.

I know a lot of teachers prefer a complicated system of phonetic practice symbols, and differentiate between open and closed Italian vowels, German vowels with and without umlauts, etc. However, in practice, the clearest, strongest, and most straightforward vowel has the best chance of surviving the

"highest" tessituras without modifying into a mere vowel-less tone.

There is no reason, when a student is taught from the beginning to use such clear vowels throughout his / her range, that the words of the Queen of the Night should not be nearly as intelligible as those of Papageno.

And since my work has been with American students, I have insisted on basic Italian sound for the vowels of all language, but illustrated these sounds with English examples, with words my students use every day; hence,

Lay, Free, Pie, No, Law, and You…

your impoverished proofer J.A.

Multiple Choices

Because the vowel exists only on the flow of the singer's psychic energy, even a raw and unfocused sounding vowel still has an elemental freedom.

A freedom unemcumbered by the inertia and torpid parasitical influences inherent in "tone production"

The student burdened with a directive to produce "tones" rather than vowels and pitches, must weigh the confusing concepts of not only Tone, but Support, Breath Control, Cover, Registers, Color, Passaggio, and Open Throat as well.

In order to have something to work with (as in any profession) these terms came into existence as if they were factual realities, endorsed in every instance by their proponents as being the one true way to achieve vocal supremacy. In time, these terms became the standard jargon of the voice teacher's profession.

Each and every alchemist of old applied the same incantations, chants, and formulas... in their bid to transmute lead into gold.

Take your pick.

Overloaded with these dictatorial concepts, both mental and physical, the student's only recourse was to experiment on his own, as to what seemed to work, and what did not.

Over the years, I have become somewhat of an iconoclast.

Bear this in mind when I tell you what does NOT work...

ALL... of the above!

The Great "Tone" God

In an ancient Aztec ritual of sacrifice, an innocent maiden's heart was ripped from her bosom.

The still beating heart, held aloft by the high priest, so captured the imagination of the populace, that they all agreed it was indeed a good thing!

Perhaps I'm too pragmatic, but I can't imagine what in hell the Gods would do with that heart. What could they possibly use it for, presuming they were interested in the first place?

The heart was the life force given by the Gods to the energy, the purity, and the mystique of its poor owner.

It had now been laid waste.

Would the "Powers That Be" really wish to kill their own creature?

If this ancient scenario bothers you for perhaps humanitarian reasons, just consider for a moment: how many singers have you know that are ready, willing, and able to kill, maim, and mutilate their sweet vowels in the name of the "Great Tone God"?

A vowel in its pure form is beautiful unto itself; it needs no pretensions of any kind. Why would anyone want to sacrifice the vowel for the "tone"? Why insist upon destroying an honest and legitimate source of sound?

(I must admit, I, too, have been guilty of this ritual)

Thou shalt not sacrifice the pure vowel by attempting to modify or convolute it to take upon itself a quality not natural to its origin!

The Dominant Vowel

One of your pure vowels will have by Mother Nature, the inherent vibrations and the stamina to outdistance all the other vowels in your voice.

This one particular vowel, regardless of its quality, is your "dominant" vowel.

Look at your hand. All your fingers work individually and, when desired, together.

What would you consider to be your dominant finger?

Now the crux of the matter...

Every singer's dominant vowel is not the same. Some will have an "EE" vowel, while in another's' voice the "AWE" vowel will reign supreme.

In my own voice, the "OH" vowel was "splendiferous"

(All the others were a motley group)

In my circle, we had one thing in common, in spite of the difference between us "structurally"

Each of us would have just loved to have had the ease and clarity of each other's dominant vowel.

(The other pasture always looks greener)

Mistaken Identity

The voice makes progress when the pure vowel, in ascending the scale, keeps its IDENTITY.

I can find no difference whatsoever between what is usually called the "tone", and the pure vowel.

How is it possible to separate the tone from the vowel, or the vowel from the tone?

Why should I even make a distinction?

Everyone (I presume) understands the function of the vowel and the mental exercise required to conjure one up; therefore, will you please explain to me, just how in hell does the "tone" remain so obnoxious a mystery?

As far as I'm concerned, the vowel, the tip of the tongue, and the consonant are the only materials you can work with... plus... your IMAGINATION!

Thy Dominant Vowel

What I call the dominant vowel in a voice is the vowel which are the most splendiferous or the most easily produced and are of a greater natural intensity for that particular student.

In my experience, any voice with a dominant "EE" or "AY", has more of a built - in or natural placement, than the student possessing a stronger or more pronounced "OH" or "AWE" vowel.

Each voice has one dominant vowel inherent in its structure.

Although the other vowels may suffer by comparison (and they do), the student instinctively knows that that vowel is the one vowel he can depend upon. Therefore, he will continue to holler out that one vowel to his heart's content.

And why not? This may be the only thing he has going for him!

This theorem is borne out by recordings some some of the "old timers" made when already past their prime.

That they lasted as long as they did was due in part to their knowledge of what their "technique" or instrument could accommodate.

Every conceivable opportunity to sing an "EE" vowel in the upper portion of his tessitura was seized upon by that great tenor Leo Slezak.

Obviously, this was his dominant vowel.

He was not alone. The other singers of the day, more often than not, also changed the text to improve their longevity.

"Any which way they could", seems to have been their credo.

And even today, the reigning prima donna's of the world are not about to allow a disagreeable consonant or vowel get in their way... and may modify it accordingly!

Rule of thumb... Thou shalt determine thy dominant vowel... even if your teacher cannot!

Renewing the Vowel

There persisted a few centuries ago an absolute belief that the world was flat. Since everyone in that day and age "knew" the world was flat, (with the possible exception of a few malcontents)... why should it be otherwise?

The problem is that everyone knows... but nobody understands!

Take the vowel for instance.

Tito Schipa was of the opinion that the vowel does not form itself inside the mouth or the throat; the vowels fall from above... over the lips, and the breath makes them run into the theater.

I can live with this. I was taught that not only are the vowels on the lips, but that one has to consciously renew them!

Renew the vowel! What kind of nonsense is this?

If your voice "goes"... why bother? Aye... there's the rub.

The vowel is not a rubber band stretching from here to eternity. It has its limits. In order to keep it alive and on the lips where it belongs, the vowel must be mentally renewed to propel it on its way.

It's simple enough. I presume we all understand that each and every word has a vowel separating the consonants. Since we must dispatch the consonant with swiftness we have only the vowel left to dwell upon.

If the vowel is not nourished mentally it loses its spontaneity.

Therefore, in order for the original vowel to prosper, it must be "reincarnated"... reinforcing itself again and again upon each and every beat in the music and upon each and every step in the scale.

It must be renewed... this is mandatory!

The Pure Vowel and Nothing But

Assuming for the moment that your AWE, AY, EE, OH, and OO vowels in the middle of your voice are somewhat secure, and about as pure as you can reasonably hope for, you or your teacher must have noticed a process of "assimilation" taking place as you ascend the scale.

This means only that the original vowel will have a tendency to change from its pure status and form a new identity in the upper portion of your tessitura.

As you rise above the staff, AWE will turn to "uh", EE to "ih", AY to "eh", OO to "uh", etc.

Although this is a natural and unavoidable phenomenon, Mother Nature will take care of any adjustments necessary.

While your teacher may be satisfied in achieving any sort of vowel above the staff (as long as the "tone" remains good)... this cannot be condoned!

No, Sir... Whatever vowel you start with ... you do your damnedest to

finish with!

Therefore thou shalt concentrate ONLY upon the vowel desired, and pay NO attention to the sound produced.

For all intents and purposes, your instrument will then deliver the "purest" vowel it can produce.

In this manner, your sweet vowel will continue to purify and improve upon itself... and any fixations upon "Tone"... will hopefully evaporate.

Birds of a Feather

Not every vowel inherent in a voice may be considered to be benign.

The two most destructive vowels (to my way of thinking) are the vowels "AH" and the vowel "EH"

In an untutored voice, these two vowels seem to flock together, intermingling to such an extent they become indistinguishable from each other.

I believe these somewhat indefinite vowels being somewhat anarchistic in nature may even conspire with each other and join forces, in an effort to produce the worst "whitish" or "nanny goat" sounds possible, seemingly in the middle of the mouth.

Far-fetched? Not really. Listen to anyone "singing" in English.

3

Covering Up

I have yet to find someone I can agree with on the precise meaning of the word "cover."

When a teacher admonishes a student for not "covering the tone", I know damn well he has no idea of what the hell he is talking about.

He doesn't know what's wrong with the "tone" the student is producing, or why it's wrong, or how to fix it.

Anyone, bar none, using this term either in a professional capacity or in a critical summation… should be shot on sight!

The only time I have used this term was to warn my students of its farcical nature as a teaching tool.

Originally, I believe, this "technique" was supposed to be a way to "open" the "passaggio" by broadening or darkening the original vowel or tone.

The majority of scales are sung on the AH vowel. The AH being the brightest of the "dark vowels" has a tendency to self-destruct in the upper portion of any instrument having a natural tendency to close up above the staff.

In order to postpone the eventual demise of this vowel, the AH vowel must be gradually darkened to assume an "OH" configuration or quality while ascending the scale.

Needless to say, the student, in trying to assimilate two differing vowels and at the same time produce the quality of "tone" desired… will also self-destruct!

"Scared Above the Staff"

This means exactly what it implies; a fear of vocal heights, (engendered in the eye of the beholder.)

The eye magnifies beyond all proportion the spaces above the staff, wherein they now become a distinct and separate part... above and beyond the normal confines of the voice.

This inordinate sense of distance or "height", transforms most tenors to jelly. A tenor contemplating G and beyond has come face to face with his worst nightmare.

His "teacher" very likely is part of the problem.

His eye is no better than his students'!

He too sees the distance or "elevation" encountered, and proceeds to admonish the student to "prepare" for the "high note"

Preparation is fine, but not the kind of preparation that involves tensing up!

Consider the fear of fire. Specifically, the age-old concept of walking

on fire.

Dangerous as this may seem, walking on fire involves nothing more... than self control! An effort of mind and will to control the sense of effort.

Specifically control of fear: a refusal to tense up!

It can be done-even by amateurs.

You must believe absolutely that you cannot be harmed, and visualize only the feeling of walking on cool... wet... grass.

I know 'tis easier said than done, but... your body will do whatever necessary to protect itself! Always has, always will.

Your larynx is no different, it will also.

The Extension Ladder Principle

Would you dare to climb an extension ladder forty eight feet high? Throwing caution to the winds, would you venture halfway up?

There you are, at the halfway mark, holding on for dear life.

Climb down to the twenty foot level and all of a sudden you will experience a vast relief; oh, my, what a difference!

However, the window to be cleaned is on the twenty five foot level, and you are not going to get anything done standing on the twenty foot level of the ladder.

What to do!

As a matter of survival, you must now climb to the thirty foot level... possibly inducing a mild case of absolute terror!

I shall now allow you to back down to the twenty-five foot level where the principle still applies... twenty five feet is so much better than thirty.

Another wave of relief ensues.

This lesson implies that you must go beyond your capabilities in order to improve.

You cannot play "safe"

You must strive for that feeling of security obtainable only by venturing above and beyond.

When you play "safe", you erect physical and psychological barriers which can only impede and weaken your resolve.

NO GUTS, NO GLORY!

"Squillo"

The most electrifying of all the sounds produced by the human throat ...and the rarest. It has been described as a primeval cry in the wilderness, wherein the voice breaks free of all constraints and issues forth as a lightning bolt from the heavens!

"Squillo" demands an absolutely free instrument for the intended pitch in the upper portion of the tessitura. Those very few tenors that possess this aural phenomena are usually forgiven any musical transgressions.

All in all, a very desirable characteristic!

The Comatose Tongue

The tongue has no desire to assume any position contrary to its nature. Prior to its first voice lesson, the tongue has enjoyed almost unlimited freedom in its inherent domain.

In speaking, your tongue may possess a tactile sense of enunciation, articulation and pronunciation, but this ambulatory activity was bred into it in a somewhat haphazardous manner from birth.

Virtuosity in verbosity is not your tongue's stock in trade!

Comatosity is more like it.

The tongue's greatest ambition is to loll around.

(Almost feline in nature)

Training the tongue to facilitate your vocal interests, is akin to training the cat to fetch your slippers. . neither of them have any interest in the proceedings!

Friend or Foe

The old cliche "Getting the Part in my Throat" is still out there, and will always be the catchword of every singer learning how to cope with his voice and the demands of the score. No subtlety here.

The instrument that must learn a role is forced to belabor itself as its owner makes a draconian attempt to "whip it into shape."

The singer fails to realize… each word of the score is unique unto itself! Damn near everything wrong with any instrument comes back to the failure of the tongue to properly articulate the consonants and observe the order in which they appear in each word.

The vowel is in essence mutilated by the tongue's inability to properly do its job.

Each and every consonant shunted aside or glossed over in any particular word or phrase will, I repeat, WILL come back to haunt you.

Never, to my knowledge, has any properly articulated consonant interfered in any way with "tone production

Now you are beginning to understand what is required. The tongue, being the only flexible muscle in your oral cavity, must be harnessed.

You can either make it your best friend… or your worst enemy.

Natural Placement

It used to be that damn near all singers, past and present, that achieved universal recognition were blessed by Mother Nature with a NATURAL PLACEMENT!

All they really knew was that their "voices" seemed to focus and regenerate themselves, without any conscious effort.

A voice without a definitive "placement" is not considered a "voice Why? Without placement, it doesn't sound like one!

A placement that sounds too "high" for the desired pitch; noticeable

physical changes occurring during changes of pitch; variations in vocal quality from note to note and vowel to vowel; obscured or "woolly" speech patterns; all are characteristics of an uneven instrument not considered to be of a uniform and consistent quality throughout its natural tessitura.

In a voice without a definitive or "natural" placement, the vowel, regardless of its purity, will, in ascending the scale, become more and more strident, and eventually self-destruct.

This is in no way a reflection upon the student's talent, intelligence, or dedication.

"Mother Nature" has simply denied this student's instrument the internal muscular freedom and agility necessary to accommodate this particular vowel any further.

Placement

Love, honor, and cherish your consonants.

Your consonant is not something to be avoided, or even to be summarily

dismissed, as is taught more often than not.

Each and every consonant, regardless of its peculiarities, is similar to the clapper on a bell.

The sympathetic vibrations induced by the tip of the tongue, in conjunction with the vowel, stimulate and reinforce the vibratory chambers of your vocal apparatus.

Specifically, forming the T, D, and N consonants, created by the action of the tip of the tongue against the ridge above your front teeth, is the only proper way to create a "Placement" within the instrument.

It does work. Any other way, to me… is a shotgun approach.

Placement

Voice "placing" is nothing more than the means used to attain the proper reflection of the vowel in the resonance chamber so that the overtones may vibrate and develop freely.

To focus the sound direct to a specific source, we use the initial contact between the tongue and the hard ridge just above the upper front teeth.

This contact is what induces the frontal vibrations so necessary to the student's sensation of placement.

This contact turns the surrounding area-including the lips, teeth and nasal cavities into "sympathetic vibrators" that enhance, complement, and amplify each other.

The consonants which initiate this contact pinpoint the center of the focus of resonance and "jar" the dormant and sleepy frontal cavities of the "Mask", into fostering added dimensions.

In doing so consonants become an "irresistible force", inducing and

seducing these immobile resonance chambers to grasp their fair share of life, liberty, and the pursuit of happiness… whether they like it or not!

The "Hum" Approach

Just about every teacher advocates "humming" as beneficial for the voice. This well may be, but not for the reasons they give.

In an attempt to induce the sympathetic vibrations of the "mask" to reverberate against the front wall of the mouth, the use of the hum, (coupled with an agreeable vowel) serves mainly to awaken a dormant or "sleepy" instrument.

It does no harm; it feels good; but it's a shotgun approach!

This "method" cannot be used (as it often is) to create a "placement", because humming stimulates too wide an area.. it does not zero in on the ridge above the front teeth; which, as I have explained before, is the center of the focus of resonance in all voices.

My Kingdom for a Consonant

I hate exercises, always did, always will.

All exercises are primarily used to improve the physical reflexes of the muscles of the larynx, to teach them to respond instinctively, and, in doing so, to lessen the lag between stimulation and response.

Of course, exercises not only help flexibility and response, they also contribute to the muscular expansion within the larynx itself.

(a prime directive here)

Having the student running an assortment of vowels up and down the scales throughout an entire lesson may make both student and teacher feel they are accomplishing a helluva whole lot... but it's not necessarily so!

What is missing is obvious.

To sing any vowel without using a consonant to propel it on its way, is the same as gunning the motor of your stalled car in the hope it will repair itself.

ALL exercises should be sung with an easily understood and forceful sentiment derived from the text of your aria.

Voice teachers, as a rule, do not agree with this approach.

They feel that, in exercises, any intrusion by the tongue must be squelched immediately... if not sooner!

The tongue, being spared the necessity of providing any motivation for the vowels' exploits, is only too happy to just loll around, doing nothing whatsoever to earn its keep.

"Ah, that's just the point", I'm now told.

However, the day will come when the student must form a consonant (in order to sing an actual text) and then all hell breaks loose!

The tongue, now forced to work for a living, is in no mood to be hustled about, and will raise all sorts of objections.

The Innocent Bystander

What is "throat"? It is the most innocent of all objects considered in the "Art of Singing" and, through no fault of its own... the most maligned and misunderstood.

As a term in the singer's vocabulary, it has been bandied about in every conceivable fashion, and used to explain whatever may go awry, for any reason whatsoever.

The defenseless throat ...is an easy target.

If I can help it at all, I make it a point to never use the word throat. This term engenders a host of imaginary problems having nothing whatsoever to do with the voice.

The throat's ONLY function... is to house the larynx!

That's it, that's all... period!

The "Open" Throat

By "pressing" down on the larynx, and "squaring" the jaw, an open throat can be achieved.

This muscular approach has its adherents, and it does work... but over a period of time, the muscular actions needed to sustain this "technique" become stiff and set in their operation. Eventually, a voice so managed can no longer produce a legato line.

Why is this?

Because this method stifles the sympathetic vibrations arising from the facial cavities; and the vowel cannot regenerate itself.

But this ain't all...

The tongue has now become a hostage!

Subordinate to the muscular strictures imposed by this "Open Throat" concept, the tongue is unable to freely perform its duties.

Therefore, without the tongue's consent, how in hell are you going to create a "Placement"?... No Can Do!

The "Float"

The "float" in the instrument is the ultimate sign of any voice's ability to soar. Having a float in no way implies any great intelligence upon the singer's part, it merely means the vocalist's instrument is inherently capable of releasing... a "tone" that then seems to "hover" and at the same time completely freeing. The float is the ultimate indication of the larynx's ability to function.

The smaller voices, especially light sopranos, more often than not possess this quality, even though it may be mismanaged.

The larger the voice, the less likely this aural phenomenon will be present. While a larger voice may be quite capable of negotiating its required tessitura, it usually always seems "pushed" or driven, rather than freed or released.

Any tension, mental or physical, often caused by demands on the voice above and beyond its working capacity, subverts the "float", although this may become apparent only over a long period of time.

Yes, I know! There were specially gifted artists of every generation who possessed this desirable quality at birth. Whether they understood what they

had as performers was a moot point.

All they really had to do was learn their parts, and shy away from all roles that would do violence to their natural voices.

However, some became teachers, even those who confessed they knew little about how they were able to do what they did.

"All I know about my method was to keep the tone from being breathy."

Alas, even performers who knew no more than that... often became

"teachers."

The Mystique of "High C"

The supreme money note. The public pays to hear it.

There were quite a few famous singers that would readily have killed to possess it. No, they had it not.

However, these singers proved to the world they could get along quite well without it.

This proves they had more going for them than more chutzpah.

But a singer who begins by having this infamous "High C" and then loses it, (the reasons are legion).. feels there is nothing on earth that can compensate for it.

Within the realm of Mother Nature, almost anything can be repaired, rebuilt, resurrected... even virginity!

Ma... a "High C"?

Careers go down the drain, suicide is contemplated, commiseration runs rampant, etc.

The performer belatedly realizes, that even transposing the music downward is no cure. The B natural still resplendent in the voice will in time, come tumbling down!

"Ah, Miseria"

Another "tonal" Misconception

The term "overtone" may be quite comprehensible to the members of an orchestra. Since they deal with them all the time, they well knoweth.

Defined as "a higher secondary tone of the basic musical tone "this ambiguous word when bandied about in the voice studio has no meaning whatsoever, in a practical sense, to the voice student.

The tendency to use the word "tone" to describe any and every sound vaguely linked to the process of singing, I find unacceptable.

Sympathetic vibrations.

Now there's a term I can get a handle on, identify with.

What are they? They are vibrations that are induced by the main vibration.

Strangely enough, (tongue in cheek here) I can even feel and sense them working for me.

The "Inner Smile" Complex

The "inner smile" concept is an attempt to induce the sympathetic vibrations of the "mask" to commingle with the "tone"

I know!... The adherents of this peculiar form of physical opening, swear by it... "It works for me"!

The singer "smiles", and supposes that thereby his soft palate has been raised, his facial resonance is standing at attention, and his "throat" is ready, willing, and able to obey his every command.

Now this would be all fine and dandy, if it worked the way it's supposed to!

However, the student, in creating this artificially contrived opening (the inner smile), never realizes he is also imposing an added burden on his voice.

While the "smile" may physically raise the soft palate, it also tightens the instrument, wherein the "pull" on the soft palate pulls the throat muscles as well.

An abnormal pressure is now being generated within his instrument, and this in turn, physically depresses the larynx, which is a No-no!

And, to add insult to injury, the performer's face freezes into the idiotic grin of one whose philosophy remains, "What... Me Worry"?

All in all, a very damaging process over a period of time.

Ultimate Resonance

I daresay that ninety-nine and one half percent of all those sincerely aspiring to better themselves - and that's only one student in two hundred! - ever achieve the true potential of what they have to work with.

Each and every voice has within its structure the essentials needed to become greater than the sum of its parts.

Strange as it may seem, even those singers most satisfied with their

"voices" do not realize they are working with an instrument delivering only

75 % of its resources... and very possibly... a helluva lot less!

(If they did, would they be satisfied? Maybe so.)

By and large, they are only too happy to keep what they've got!

Nasal Resonance

Nasal resonance is a woefully misunderstood form of vibration.

Unfortunately, as far as the average voice student is concerned, cultivating this facet of the voice falls far below his or her immediate priorities.

Her teacher does not concern himself with something he does not

understand. To him "it's all in the mask", whatever the hell the "mask" may consist of.

The singer in question may reasonably assume "If I do not sound "nasal" (indicating a closed nasal reservoir) I must be singing with an "open nasal resonance!"

Not necessarily so.

The "sympathetic" vibrations "responding" within the rest of the voice, may well disguise the voice in such a way as to make the lack of nasal resonance... barely discernable.

What's the difference?

Very subtle, but still a helluva whole lot!

The vocal apparatus, in adding to its resources the darker - colored vibrations of the nasal passages, not only modifies and gives a warmer quality to the vowel, but enhances the feeling of placement within the voice itself.

Thou Shalt Open Thy "Sniffer"! This is mandatory.

The "Lifting Process"

Due to a fortunate combination of circumstances (for the singer) sometimes a voice will "transfer" itself to a higher tessitura i.e. (mezzo to soprano). The voice is now acknowledged to have "lifted"

What has really happened, of course, is that the singer was previously performing in a tessitura lower than the natural inclination of the instrument.

When the soprano found out she was a soprano, and not a basso, everything became a lot easier!

"Misdiagnosed" is too polite a term.

One day, I hope to hear of a court case, wherein the student so dealt with... (i.e. made to sing in a lower-than-natural tessitura by a lazy or ignorant teacher)... got her money back!

4

Abuse

Pianissimo

Amplitude

"Chest Voice"

Out of Range

Born Free

"Color"

Bigger is Better

The Basso "Illegitimus"

A Soft Thought

Falsetto

The "Singhiozzo"

Muscular Meditation

Perfect Pitch

Buried Treasure

Vibrato

"Breaking Out"

Trickling Down

Abuse

A symbiotic relationship exists between you and your instrument.

From the day you emerged from the womb and shook the rafters, your voice has always striven to achieve whatever you have demanded of it.

Aye... there's the rub!

If any part of your body could be considered to have suffered cruel and unusual punishment, 'tis indeed your larynx!

Over the years these demands invariably take their toll; this trusting and loyal partner of yours...can now no longer please you!

Those in ignorance of the true reasons behind its demise will assume you "lost" your voice.

Naturally the performer's ego would never permit him to admit (even in privacy) that perhaps (with the best intentions in the world) he did on occasion use more force than necessary; created a greater tension than called for; possibly even undue atmospheric pressure was generated... and now his instrument, in order to comply with these excessive demands, has assumed a position

detrimental to its health!

"Bent all out of shape

Try hitting your finger with a hammer.

How many blows can you inflict... before your finger raises an objection?

I've always felt, that if your instrument could hire a lawyer.. you would take much better care of it.

Pianissimo

A famous soprano has stated; "You either have the capacity to love, or you do not; and you are either born with a pianissimo, or you are not!"

I believe this.

A reduced mezzavoce is not a pianissimo.

The capacity within the instrument to spin out this aural phenomena in the uppermost part of the tessitura is (I believe) a gift from Mother Nature.

Don't fret! You can get along quite well without it.

A mezzavoce is an excellent substitute, and it CAN be cultivated.

Amplitude

The inherent potential of anyone's instrument, depends almost entirely upon what voice teachers consider a "voice."

Even to the untrained ear, a voice devoid of "amplitude" does not qualify.

Those born without it (me included) strive for years to bring the voice to some semblance of approval.

Any student gifted by Mother Nature with a voice that "goes", will obviously have a much easier road to travel. What he's got going for him is an ease of tessitura without undue restraint. Whether his voice has any endearing qualities attached to it is of secondary importance. The voice travels... anything else can be "ironed out"

Whether he understands anything at all as to how or why he was blessed in this manner, or even cares... is a moot point.

In spite of the freedom inherent in the muscular structure of his instrument, giving his voice the amplitude necessary to negotiate the required tessitura without physical or psychological restraint... this in no way guarantees this student a definitive placement.

"Chest" Voice

I don't know how this snake-oil term originated, but since most singers pretend to understand what it means and how it works, I won't argue the point.

To me "chest" voice implies that there must be a completely separate set of vocal cords residing elsewhere in the body.

Since we all know this isn't so, why not call these "chest tones" what they really are?

That is: an unnatural contortion of the vocal apparatus, used by some singers to artificially induce and produce a big "tone" in their "lower register"

The only time I have ever used this term was to acquaint my students with the drawbacks of the practice it described.

Out of Range

At the other end of the spectrum, any imbalance within the instrument caused by inborn muscular tensions (a lack of amplitude) will always cause a "discordant placement." Without a definitive placement, the voice is understood to be... "out of whack."

One tenor once told me, "you're not high enough"

I thought I knew what he meant... but neither of us understood what the hell we were talking about!

This vagueness about where bad placement comes from has led to the erroneous assumption that the vocal apparatus must contain within itself several boundary layers... registers!

Depending upon your teacher's preference, you may be saddled with as many as four!

To reunite these unequal resonance "chambers" into a unified whole will occupy the attention of teacher and student for years to come.

This assumption is based on another assumption: that this student's teacher knows what the hell he is doing... otherwise, all bets are off!

Meanwhile, the student, having no choice in the matter, must learn to "shift gears" between registers... in order to bring forth his "high notes"!

Eventually... a very few... do get lucky...

Why should anyone have more registers than a canary?

He does wonders with the one he has!

Born Free

A canary, or any songbird for that matter, has not the slightest interest in how his vocal apparatus functions.

Why should he?

Unburdened by the lunacy practiced by others on the planet, he blithely chirps away.

He does have one tremendous advantage going for him though.

Nowhere in his repertoire is he required to form a consonant!

"Color"

A good impressionist can, through body movement, good material, and ingeniously manipulated vocal resources, establish well over half a hundred "colorful" personalities.

Within the limited tessitura he works in, he mentally induces his instrument to conjure up what is required.

But... nowhere is he required to sing!

Now, there's a horse of a different color.

Contrary to all accepted beliefs... you cannot "color" a "tone" through voluntary physical action. Such "coloring" leads to only one thing... distortion within the instrument.

If you wish to convolute your voice in this manner, so be it!

However, you need not. All you really have to do to achieve "color", is to believe implicitly in what you are saying. Nothing more, nothing less.

In any spoken conversation, the voice will assume the emotions desired.

Witness a good domestic argument!

Bigger is Better

Ask any singer:

"Do you know whether the size of the vowel, in any singer's voice, is proportional to the size of the singer's upper lip?

A blank stare is the immediate response. (Whah?)

(Hell, I don't know either!)

However, if you visualize the vowel on your upper lip to be the size of a basketball... wonders occur.

Holding an imaginary basketball between your two outstretched palms

does the job.

In this manner, you tend to magnify the vowel beyond its natural state wherein it now becomes... "augmented"

Conversely, the consonant, in order to interrupt the vowel and not do it violence, must be considered to be about the size of your little fingernail.

The Basso "Illegitimus"

True to their calling, all basses are morbidly attracted to the quality of the "tones" skulking about in the lower regions of their tessitura, and naturally assume the only proper way to "sing" them would be to imitate the sounds made by other basses, usually on recordings.

This impulsive urge to sing along is quite normal.

While I may applaud the manner in which the recording artist of his choice maintains the musical line, interpretive nuances, style, diction, phrasing, etc. I will dissuade (in no uncertain terms) any attempt by the student to duplicate the basic color or timbre inherent in any other voice than his own.

No instrument is capable of sustaining this abuse, and this is far and away the most destructive of all the rituals imposed upon it.

Balky, defiant, and even mutinous at times, your larynx still has the good sense to recognize and defy any attempt to meld, mold, or alienate its instinctive desire to propagate itself and its own quality, and will take a very dim view of any affront to its natural proclivity.

Imitation may be the sincerest form of flattery, but your larynx has no desire to be... anybody else's!

Why kill the goose that lays the golden eggs?

A Soft Thought

A "soft" thought leads to soft singing. (mezzavoce)

Although some voices may be more amenable and better suited in carrying out the performer's wishes in this respect, it's not easy for anyone.

For soft singing a full resonance is vital.

You must learn how to turn down the physical intensity of your voice by lowering the mental intensity... without reducing the resonance or the size of the vowel.

Under no circumstances do you ever conceive a vowel to be small.

The tyranny of this "piano" too often inspires an undernourished vowel lacking in brilliance and carrying power.

A muffled or "smeared" vowel is created when the mind confuses the term "softer" with "less intense"

Falsetto

I believe that the falsetto mechanism within the larynx can be cultivated to assume a preeminent role in any singer's repertoire.

I won't pretend to understand just how it functions and why some singers have the ability to command its presence... I know I didn't. Bass, baritone or tenor, it matters not, falsetto plays no favorites.

Do not confuse this thin and hollow sound with the hooty "tonal frontal" which is a limited and raw, forced "head tone"

In ascending the scale, the vowel (each one unique in its own way) will inevitably reach the point of no return.

The vocal apparatus, unable to sustain the pressures involved, and unable to make any further adjustments within itself to sustain the original concept; "breaks" and a falsetto "tone" appears.

Now this shifting of gears is a natural protective device within the larynx, and there is nothing wrong with it.

Some teachers call this phenomena a change of registers.

I don't. To my way of thinking, the falsetto is part and parcel of the whole ball of wax, and must be harnessed.

Every instrument has within itself not only the capacity to achieve its ultimate resonance, but also its ultimate tessitura.

The "Singhiozzo"

Singhiozzo is the Italian word for "sob." It is also a vocal term, and is applied to voices which have such a rich physical quality of emotion that they seem to contain a "sobbing" sound as part of their natural resonance or timbre.

Joseph Schmidt, Rosa Ponselle, Beniameno Gigli. These singers were especially noted for the "Tear" or "Sigh" in their voice.

There are very few blessed with this unique quality which is inherent within the instrument. Even these especially gifted voices, however, cannot, by any stretch of the imagination, hope to escape the drudgery of learning the "How, Why and Wherefore" of the way things work in professional singing.

Granted, their voices will always attract attention, but a career... demands integrity!

Muscular Meditation

(While U Wait)

A student "gifted" by Mother Nature with an instrument that complies generously with the demands made upon it will bypass most of the learning procedures inflicted upon his less fortunate brethren.

Since his voice seems to respond in a cooperative fashion, why should he question any of his teacher's precepts?

In every vocal apparatus there exists a muscle memory response.

The muscular "lag" between stimulation and response within the larynx is almost entirely responsible for the frustration among those plagued with an instrument that just doesn't "go"

The student who, through no fault of his own is forced to contend with a balky instrument eventually reaches a compromise wherein what he wants is reconciled with what his larynx can deliver.

What no one understands... is the time element involved!

Based upon my own vocal shortcomings I believe that the muscular memory response of the larynx is anywhere between twelve and fifteen months... AFTER the initial mental commands have been implemented... before it can subconsciously obey them.

Of course I can't prove this... and I'm not about to argue the point, but... think about it?

Perfect Pitch

Some have it, some don't. Don't fuss, you don't need it.

If this were not so, who in hell would be singing all the parts?

All singers (the diligent ones anyway) reach a level of competency wherein they become quite proficient in identifying a pitch "relatively"

Once a certain pitch has been identified, even the hard of hearing have no trouble figuring out and correlating the rest of the notes "relative" to it.

"Tune deaf" people cannot discriminate between a series of correct notes sung in a song, or those sung inaccurately.

Both of these rare attributes, perfect pitch and tune-deafness, note I did not say tone-deafness, are nearly always inherited.

Buried Treasure

Mother Nature (by her very nature) demands freedom... but not always to your advantage.

Since emerging from the confines of the cradle, your vocal instrument has been besieged by layers of fear and self doubt, that in turn... subconsciously stifle and inhibit its functions, in order to serve and protect.

Though these patterns of denial and self-preservation may well have saved your ass from all kinds of lawsuits, they contribute nothing whatsoever to the health and well-being of your instrument.

Your true vocal resources, may indeed, be buried under a mountain of emotional debris.

Vibrato

This tremulous or "quivering" effect caused by the very rapid partial interruptions of the pure vowel is a natural and inherent attribute of the vocal instrument embellishing the natural quality or timbre of the voice.

If your voice does not pulsate, throb, or have this vibrato in motion, you are singing incorrectly.

Under tension, some unduly dark or heavy vocal instruments will sound dull or under pitch, whereas a "white" voice (read: tight instrument) will have practically no vibrato at all.

A word of warning; Do not attempt to control, augment, or diminish its capacity in any way. Leave it Alone!

"Breaking Out"

It is a natural law that sooner or later, the muscular apparatus within and surrounding the student's instrument will suffer... a nervous breakdown.

No longer able to forestall the student's determined assault upon its territory (and perhaps with a sigh of resignation), the larynx will "throw in the towel" ... and offer no further resistance.

Always unprepared for this benign feeling of physical amnesty, the startled student, now freed for the moment of all constraints, finds his voice spontaneously regenerating itself, with an ease and freedom unmatched by his previous efforts.

Biding its time, and patiently gathering its resources, your larynx will adapt to this new configuration within itself .. but it is not about to give up all the bad habits of a lifetime!

Trickling Down

After a period of time, every student will inevitably discover that one vowel in his voice that defies every attempt to harness it.

Through no fault of his own, he is saddled with a vowel that, when called upon, becomes balky, mulish, and just plain stubborn!

Naturally, he dreads singing it.

In life and love, opposites attract. In a singer's voice, however, the "dominant" vowel will hold no courtship with his undernourished neighbors, preferring instead to remain aloof, and above his colleagues.

What to do?

We now proceed to lavish all kinds of tender loving care upon the dominant vowel, giving him all the consideration he deserves.

When the dominant vowel feels itself becoming bigger, stronger, and better "placed" this encourages the other weaker vowels to share his residual sympathetic vibrations, and they, in turn, being nurtured by this process... will also prosper!

Your dominant vowel is not troubled at all by this arrangement.

In his own way he relishes this preferential treatment.

However, the day will come when he can no longer dominate his brethren, and ultimately... accepts them as his equals.

(You may consider all this as a trickle - down theory... it works!)

5

Voice Students • Voice Teachers • and other Wild Beasts

Love Me Tender

Minimum Standards

On a Scale of 1 to 10

Mirror, Mirror on the Wall

On the Road Again

The Child of Nature

Implied Expertise

Before the Dawn of Singing Teachers

"Garble Garble"

Interpretation

The Security Blanket

Old Mountain Proverb

The Astute Student's Dilemma

Minimum Requirements

The Learning Process

The Good, the Bad, and the Ugly

Quack Quack

Lend Me Your Ears

Narcissus? Who He?

The "lower" Common Denominator

The Artful Codger

Love Me Tender

I can aid you in your quest for divine fulfillment. My method of Transformational Singing will enable you to embark upon a musical journey into parts of the voice and the self one doesn't normally use.

My students are taught in a non stressful therapeutic atmosphere of tender loving care. Rest assured, I shall never invade your comfort zone, lower your self esteem or chastize the child within you.

I allow you to chose the magic bell sound that best expresses your emotions and character thereby empowering your personality to create the technique to affirm the natural harmonic range of your voice. In doing so we bypass the mundane drudgery, the angst and anxiety coupled with loss of esteem, to still the inner critic and free your natural creative flow, whereas you can now surrender your inner voice to those sensations engendered by the child within you.

Minerva Peabody

S.P.C. to V.T.

Tarot Card Traveler through Time and Space

Spiritualist of the Cosmic Creations and Cremations Society.

Minimum Standards

Do You Have the "Right Stuff"?

A student's personality plays a far greater part in his pursuit of vocal culture than most students realize.

There are a half dozen personality traits absolutely essential to your survival. All of them are of equal importance.

You must be…

Willing to work. Without the willpower and self-control to hurdle the pitfalls and unravel the complexities involved, you will never make progress.

Willing to take chances? You damned well better be. You cannot play "safe No guts… no glory!

Willing to compete. Without it, you will never gain a foothold anywhere. How are you ever going to win a scholarship, a contest, or an audition?

Willing to cooperate. Congeniality. Whether you like it or not, you cannot sing solo. You will meet and have to sing with people you would not sit next to on a crowded lifeboat!

Willing to concentrate. Can you zero in on your target? Do you get flustered easily? Does your attention wander?

Willing to trust yourself. Self-confidence. How ambitious are you? Are you willing to give your all? How much of a positive viewpoint do you have?

Willing to criticize yourself. (I know… this hurts the most!)

On a Scale of 1 to 10

Just how good a student are you? Would you lie to whatever Deity you pay homage to? You say no? Well then… why lie to yourself?

No fudging allowed.

****

10- Nearer my God to thee.

9- "Lordy, I really do try!"

8- "I can't really practice as much as I should, but I do practice more than I used to."

7- "It's just one thing after another - the flu, my allergies, my female afflictions… but in between all these disabilities I practice as hard as I can."

6- "I know I screw off a lot, but, I really do put in a lot of time practicing, sometimes… even in the shower."

5- "My voice is very fragile, and I will not do anything to impair or frighten it."

4- "Hey, gimme a break! I've only had four teachers, and none of them was smarter than I was."

3- "I'm just taking lessons to impress my friends."

2- Standard Liar, Cheater, and Poltroon.

1- Miserable Polecat

****

Enlisting in any branch of the service, you learn one thing: discipline. It is drilled into you whether you like it or not.

Self-discipline (in the absence of a sergeant) is proportional to your desire to succeed.

The Less you have, The Longer it takes.

(you have my permission… to either burn, or eat this page)

Mirror, Mirror, on the Wall...

"All I wanted to do was sing a few show tunes... I didn't know it was going to be this much trouble!"

The dilettante habitually sings in "pretty", and in extreme cases "dialect", wherein I suspect they do not wish to be understood! Tone is the most important password in their vocabulary.

The true dilettante will never consider a lack of knowledge to be a disadvantage. This vainglorious purveyor of the arts will never attempt to ask, inquire, or communicate with someone who may possibly know more than she does.

Any questions of a technical nature directed to her will induce a vagueness impossible to penetrate... the eyes glaze over. You may as well have asked a Rotweiler to adopt a homeless kitten!

An almost "holier than thou" attitude shields this tourista in her quest for Artistic Divinity.

Nothing can be permitted to intrude upon her self esteem. Any one daring to cast aspersions upon her... will never be forgiven.

Of course this individual may realize her teacher is nothing more than a servile flatterer, but this suits her just fine.

Like any fluffy creature, she just loves being "stroked"

The dilettantes of the world may not imagine themselves to be better than others, it's more a case of "there are other singers?"

They are lifelong members of the Critics Anonymous Club.

Their most wished-for dream... to hobnob with the crowned heads of the opera world.

The ultimate fate of the dilettante is not unlike that of Narcissus who so admired his own beauty and grace, that he eventually fell into the pond and drowned.

To put it bluntly, these dabbler's have their heads up their asses.

On the Road Again

Two students met while attending a performance at the opera.

One student proudly confessed to the other that he was now studying with a genuine "Maestro." He had been "Reborn"

The other student allowed as to having been vocally reborn, five times!

He also implied that, while it was quite obvious that no one teacher could teach him everything he needed to know; however, the teacher he was studying with now knew everything!

Student No.1

"Oh Wow… like what?"

Student No.2

"Well, like you have to support the tone with the breath, and cover the vowel with the resonance, and combine them both in such a way as to have the tone exit through the mouth, the vowel through the nose, so that they both join together on the lips."

Student No. 1

[Awe-struck at the Implications of this Revelation]

"I didn't know that

Student No.2

"Well… when you've been around as many teachers as I have, you soon get to know it all!"

The Child of Nature

There's one cliche in the music world that I feel to be without any merit whatsoever. It not only excuses the performer from any negative criticism…but actually condones his slip-shod modus operandi as a force to be understood and admired.

"I sing from the heart"!

Well, that explains everything… no wonder you're all choked up!

Take two aspirins and call me in the morning.

Implied Expertise

Yes it's true...

A great singer does not always make a great teacher.

One of the great bassos of this century admits quite honestly to not knowing how the instrument works and therefore he does not claim to be a voice teacher. He is, without a doubt, a superb musical coach.

Sticking to what he can do for a pupil and avoiding what he can't, he

continues to be an asset to the singing world.

A stentorian tenor from a bygone era, a very great artist, but less rich in

self-knowledge than our basso, did teach voice.

His reputation was such, that every denizen in the tenor domain came out of the woodwork, hoping to study with him.

However, his "method" left a lot to be desired.

The weaker or more delicate voices were swept into oblivion, and those pupils astute enough to realize what was going on got out while they still could.

With this teacher, you either survived his "method" or he broke your voice.

Those students that did survive, carried on his precepts, and in turn broke the voices of their students.

A lifetime of experience driving an automobile does not in any way qualify you as an auto mechanic!

And, rest assured, you may also be one of those incapable of teaching

someone else how to drive!

Before the Dawn of Singing Teachers

A motley group of bystanders are gazing at an ominous cloud hovering above them.

"Son, that is without a doubt, the spirit of your mother-in-law!"

"Really? So that's why it looks like a wild bull moose."

"Oh, oh, I hear thunder; she must be grumbling about something."

"It looks awfully green around the edges; it must be made of cheese."

"Made of cheese? How many times must I tell you? Only the moon is made of cheese!"

"Hey, you numquids... don't you know anything? It floats, only feathers float."

"Oh, oh... that means only one thing; she's going to dump on us!"

(they all scatter in different directions)

"Garble Garble"

So, how do the ideas of "singers of repute" become so variable, destructive and confusing?

All students acquire the knowledge of their preferred craft or trade from a Higher Authority.

On the strength of this teaching, they go on to become Higher Authorities themselves.

In my heyday as a window cleaner, I continuously modified the knowledge and the skills acquired to suit my own particular talents and temperament.

However, I soon learned... that in order to survive... some rules were

never to be broken.

Not all singers remember the basic, unchanged principles as they originally learned them - or remember even how those principles changed when applied by themselves to their own voices.

All too often, in singing, a third-or forth-generation Higher Authority is presenting, as the unchanged, age old basics of "Bel Canto", ideas that have become strained, distorted, misapplied, or even, at times, directly opposed to its original concept.

Interpretation

Every singer wants to do it "My Way."

Good... more power to you!

However, I firmly believe "interpreting" to be the source from which most vocal faults originate and proliferate.

Aided, abetted, and approved by the teachers, coaches and other functionaries at hand, the poor student, who is hard enough pressed to keep a semblance of vocal consistency, must also bear the added burden of dramatizing his material.

An incomplete (read: student) instrument is just not resilient enough to be abused in this manner.

Whole schools of "singing" based upon nothing more than this "delivery system" shall always be with us.

Even an instrument capable of transmitting the desired emotional impact will not always be in the best state of health afterwards.

This is a major reason why the "old timers" rested their voices after a strenuous performance, even to the extent of communicating in sign language!

Even Maria Callas (as much as I loved her) went far beyond the measure of her instrument's ability to bear up under this punishing ritual, and exhausted her vocal resources in her persistent quest for the ultimate interpretive values.

The Security Blanket

After an arduous practice session, the two combatants involved both agree that some progress has been made, and a lot accomplished.

As they parted, (both a little the worse for wear), the vocalist promises his accompanist that he will refine and strengthen his interpretation... when he has the piece in question memorized!

This charade has been going on for years. This character never gets his nose out of the score! His musicianship is about as substantial as quicksand.

No matter what transpires between them, the day will never come when this dilettante will "wing it", let the chips fall where they may, and give a performance without his "security blanket"

Old Mountain Proverb

"A man will walk into hell with his eyes wide open, but even the devil can't fool a dog"

Why is it that we brush aside our survival instincts and delude ourselves into entering a fantasy world of no real substance?

I have met some pretty dense "students" in my time.

Without exception, they will embrace any statement about singing communicated to them by any singer of repute no matter how far-fetched or incomprehensible it may seem.

If the teacher attempts to question or even dissuade the student from accepting the statements of such a singer as inviolable truths, the student will then proceed to extol the virtues of this particular singer and summarily dismiss any contrary or conflicting viewpoints.

When you run across someone who sounds rather "bedraggled" or has "lost his voice", you may find him to be one of those numerous unfortunates that embrace all suggestions... rather than selecting what may seem to work for them and throwing out what they cannot use.

These students cannot separate or reconcile conflicting ideas and become hopelessly confused.

The Astute Student's Dilemma

There are also those students who are uncommonly astute.

They may begin with no conception of the mechanics of singing, but their gut instinct and common sense rise to the fore.

When they don't understand a direction, when a fancy figure of speech makes no sense, or when something they've been told to do isn't producing the desired result - or worse, is producing the opposite result, they ask questions.

The "Maestro", when questioned, invariably responds with a vague summary of inconsequential beliefs... never really understanding what the student's question meant.

Mental "dry rot" has set in.

The horror implied here is that the "Maestro" does not want to understand; he is rooted to his ill-founded beliefs!

In any field of endeavor, the truths greatest enemy has always been the myths perpetrated by the ignorant or the unconscionable adherents of their craft.

Minimum Requirements

I know I am in the minority of vocal teachers when I profess to believe that those unfortunate students that at first hearing, seem untalented, out of tune, possessing a mediocre instrument of dubious quality and range... can still make their mark!

All swans began as ugly ducklings.

Whether a potential student has a "voice" or not, makes no difference to me.

The less he has to work with, the bigger the challenge.

The only thing I ask for, is that he be musical and love music.

But, and this is a big but... he must also assure me, in no uncertain terms that he is willing to take direction, bust his ass, go the extra mile, sweat blood, practice diligently, etc.

Otherwise, he might as well seek out those teachers (and they abound) who will praise him, promise untold dividends, and fail to spread the word to one and all of his unique qualifications.

I've got better things to do than pander and pamper.

The Learning Process

On the other end of the scale, there are students who, in allowing their emotions to overcome their common sense, do not seem to learn either from reading or being told!

(The school systems bear me out on this.)

Such singers seem to "feel" that only by their own experience and mistakes can they grasp any of the principles they are being taught and learn how to use them.

If your ego dominates your brain pan... why study with a teacher?

A pre-teenager sought my advice on how to build a low winged, rubber powered model airplane.

After explaining everything in detail, I left him on his own.

Checking on his progress a week later, I questioned him as to why he had built... two left wings!

The look on his face told me that from then on... he would study the plans, follow the directions, and do what was necessary.

The Good, the Bad, and the Ugly

As happens with other organized gangs, voice teachers tend to band together for mutual support, admiration and esteem.

The good, the bad, and the ugly proliferate.

Now each and every member of the fraternity knows at least one fellow member… whose brain has atrophied.

This slight hindrance will in no way affect his teaching prowess.

Frozen in his concepts, he is free now of responsibility to himself and to others, and, rest assured, he will never be tainted or swayed by common sense… or any other such nonsense!

In order to preserve peace, prosperity, and themselves, none amongst them would dare to cast the first stone.

In doing so, such a breacher of etiquette would himself be subject to scrutiny, and heaven forbid… this is to be avoided at all costs!

This close-knit group does have one thing in common… generous to a fault, they modestly agree that one could not know everything; but, each in his own way… knows as much as humanly possible!

Quack Quack

In order to determine what a student has going for her, or what she's got to work with, voice teachers, as a rule, apply their golden rule. Hedge all bets! If she looks like a duck, squats like a duck, quacks like a duck, well hell… she's a duck!

How could she be otherwise?

However, over a period of time, and due solely to her teacher's astute and all-encompassing vocal knowledge, this ugly duckling is beginning to blossom… into a full-blown swan!

Amazingly enough, even though all the other creatures of the forest instinctively knew that this ugly duckling was a swan to begin with, rest assured, this teacher will take full credit for the transformation!

(If on the other hand, the ugly duckling grows up an ugly duck, the teacher will take no blame.)

"Well, I warned her she was just a duck!"

Lend Me Your Ears

Damned near every student I've ever known… kept his own counsel.

Why is it that voice students cannot permit themselves to seek out and either parlay or practice with other students of their own caliber? In a word… the fear of disapproval.

There seems to be some self-defense mechanism dominated by your ego, that by its very nature forbids you to accept or even expose yourself to criticism or comments by anyone working on your own level.

More's the pity, because students, more than anyone, should realize the beneficial results of comparing "notes" with one another.

An extra pair of sympathetic ears can do wonders.

As a student everyone I bummed around with was privy to each other's vocal problems and the possible solutions we could employ.

Being young and idealistic we pooled our resources and were more than happy to listen to each other, although not always harmoniously.

But, to a man, each and every one of us knew of another student who in turn became progressively worse.

What is implied here, is that no matter how compassionate and sincere your exhortations… they usually fall upon deaf ears!

My co-conspirators of old understood there was no shame involved.

Since we all stunk… we were all in the same boat!

Narcissus? Who He?

I have discovered a premise that had taken me years to understand.

After much soul searching, I now realize… the two greatest singers in the world are (modesty forbids me) and the last singer I happened to speak to!

Others, much more astute than I am… knew this instinctively.

The "lower" Common Denominator

Whatever the voice category (Fach) you belong to (or think you do) it's all the same when it comes to being paid.

You are paid for your "high notes" only!

This is the major reason why singers afflicted with more than their share

of vocal problems resort to singing roles unsuited to their instrument's natural tessitura.

Any voice that does not immediately fit a certain category, its true nature or tessitura being somewhat occluded, runs the risk of being relegated to a lower

"register."

Now, any teacher not certain of the true vocal potential of the student... automatically plays "safe"

I say this, because there are more sopranos being "trained" as mezzos, baritones as basses, etc., than you can shake a stick at!

I lost a potential scholarship in New York... only because of my insistence I was a tenor, and not the baritone the consensus of opinions implied!

Perhaps I should have "faked it"... but I could not in good conscience study with any teacher that lacked the perception necessary to evaluate a voice such as mine.

Any singer, whether by choice or design, knowingly singing lower than their natural tessitura... is flirting with DISASTER!

The Artful Codger

Every once in a while, a teacher will find on his doorstep another self-appointed answer to his prayers.

This penny-pinching schemer imagines that any teacher he approached would and should bestow upon him the tender loving care he so richly deserves, and that the teacher, overwhelmed with gratitude, would bless the day they found each other... with no mention of recompense whatsoever.

After all, why should someone so "gifted" have to pay?

Now this teacher has also been around the block a few times.

He well knows that this grifter's greatest gift is... a pair of Brass Balls!

6

The Industrious Dabbler

Unlawful Entry

A Sacred Cow's Assumption

Terminology

Voice Teacher's Exhortations

Breaking the Sound Barrier

A Doubtful Advantage

Credentials

Short - Changers

Fools are More to be Feared than the Wicked

The Odds are Not in your Favor

Teachers

Diplomatic Immunity

The Bug Brigade

Evaluating Your Ego

They do it "Their Way"

?

Love Me, Love My Voice

The Whole Truth and Nothing But...

The Dark Side of the Spectrum

Those who know more than those who know nothing

Modesty "Personified"

The Industrious Dabbler

The dictionary defines "Technique" as "a skill acquired by a thorough mastery of the subject."

In all the years I've cleaned windows, never once have I ever heard that word mentioned... there was no need for it.

I knew exactly what to do... and how to do it.

Ah, but in the "Art of Singing"..."technique" has been bastardized to include every conceivable concept ever brought to bear on the subject.

And why not?

The Deep Significance of this term brings to many of those with a good natural voice and a convincing style of delivery a sense of well being and accomplishment... far beyond what is justified by any particular knowledge of their craft.

What they really mean to say (but haven't the courage) is that their particular "style" or delivery system, is the modus operandi behind it all... but that would of course infer a lack of technical expertise... and that would hardly be conductive to their self-esteem.

Yes... they teach too!

Unlawful Entry

It has been said that the psychiatric profession cannot be considered a science because "it derives no laws." Now, no one can deny that psychiatrists are very adept at offering explanations in hindsight. Big deal!

How about predicting something that will happen!

In common with this rationale, the "science" of voice teaching also originates no new laws... except of course, those offered up by its practitioners... who dispel whatever "laws" they may be conjuring up at the moment... with varying degrees of success...

Based upon their common sense, folk wisdom, and their own experience in the field, voice teachers present to the uninitiated student a most plausible explanation of any and all theories they may embrace at the moment.

But whatever concepts any voice teacher may advocate, rest assured that he or she feels more than equal to the task of teaching them to you, and of course, more than equal to any other voice teacher you ever had or ever will have.

A Sacred Cow's Assumption

The music world abounds with propositions deemed to be self- evident.

One of the most pernicious is that no voice can be "built up"

This is based on the assumption that if you are not "born with it"... forget it!

No ninety-seven pound weakling could ever hope to enter the ring and gain championship status... so why bother?

A "Maestro" may not dissuade those students obviously lacking the required attributes, but he will let them know they have a "rocky" road to

travel, and well may be wasting their time and money.

(The honest ones anyhow)

Now, the Maestro's appraisal of a student's potential may well stem from the fact that the maestro himself was "born with" a voice.

Therefore, he himself has doubts about the value of teaching something he thinks is a "gift"

Understand that, and don't take his attitude to heart!

More often than not, the most "gifted" know the least.

After all, they needed, and received... the least teaching!

Terminology

The vocabulary peculiar to the vocal apparatus and the "Art" of singing is such a hodgepodge of conflicting terms that even those who understand precisely what they mean to say have difficulty in communicating with each other.

To my knowledge, no other "Science" has such a mishmash of aphorisms, maxims, and mysticism ingrained in its terminology.

I will not deny that the teacher is dealing in intangibles, (that which

cannot be touched or grasped) and therefore, each in his own way attempts to parlay his "expertise" so as to make the student understand what is presumably occurring.

Now the mythology perpetrated by the advocates of "Bel Canto" comes not so much from ignorance, but from their lack of knowing and understanding precisely how and why the voice works the way it does.

Voice Teacher's Exhortations

Imagine if you will, how to…

"Open your resonance."

(Would a hole in the head help?)

"Keep your throat narrow."

(Would a noose help?)

"I want a lower throat."

(What's he think I am, a pelican?)

"Don't let your throat get away from you."

(I'll put it on a leash.)

"You are not supporting."

(I may need a bigger jock strap.)

"Open your passaggio."

(Don't get personal.)

"You are not drinking the sound; vowel; etc."

(I haven't got a glass.)

"The tone is not in the Mask; Box; etc."

(Should I gift wrap it?)

"Place the tone; vowel; etc. higher."

(Would a frontal lobotomy help?)

"You must have the tone on the breath, not behind it."

(Maybe I should just mime everything.)

"Keep that egg in the back of your throat"

(It might be a lot easier to just lay one.)

"You are not floating the tone, make the tone soar."

(Oh, if I had the wings of an angel.)

The less your teacher understands about your vocal instrument, the more he is forced to apply… the foggy aphorisms of his trade.

Breaking the Sound Barrier

The Glowworm's Dictum: "When you gotta glow... you gotta glow."

When you gotta practice... you gotta practice!

My voice was quite similar to the sound and fury of a bagpipe player.

It was very difficult to prove whether either of us had improved.

Run-ins with the landlord, the neighbors, people in the park across the street, and even the gendarmes, will always challenge the self-esteem and tenacity of any singer... whose voice breaks the sound barrier.

Wherever and whenever I sang, the local termites immediately sought refuge elsewhere.

The chaos thus created, is inversely proportional to the quality of the instrument. As your voice improves... the complaints lessen.

If you do not offend someone, in some way, as a beginner, you are not going to make progress.

In an eyeball to eyeball confrontation, you must arouse your predatory instincts... Hold Your Ground!

P.S. You might imply, that you also play the Banshee...

what would they prefer?

A Doubtful Advantage

A singer's insight into how his voice works, and why, need bear no relation whatsoever to his ability to play a musical instrument.

Although my friends and I all had a great talent for honking horns and ringing doorbells... that was the best we could manage.

Even the challenge of learning to play the harmonica was beyond our talents.

In retrospect, this might even have worked to our advantage!

Since the music did not come easily to any of us, we all sweated blood trying to hurdle each musical obstacle and assemble what we needed to know. Strange as it may seem, we never felt "disadvantaged"

We even, at times, felt smugly superior to those that could play an instrument, but could not sing!

Hey... we had to compensate somehow!

Credentials

Each and every voice teacher will of financial necessity (and perhaps for ego gratification) humbly boast of their flawless perfection in the field.

A self-defense mechanism!

What a teacher may have once accomplished as a singer, pianist, or conductor, the laurels then bestowed upon his brow, is to me... of no consequence!

My only concern, is whether his presumed technical expertise and the ability to impart it... are valid.

We're talking voice here! I am not interested in studying with someone well-versed in stagecraft, conducting, makeup, interpretation, chorale litany, etc. who uses this as an alternative or makeshift background for vocal credentials.

Short - Changers

Because the introspective student does not take everything at face value, he has always posed a threat to any practitioner with dubious credentials.

The teacher in question does not want to match wits with anyone over his presumed dominance in the field.

He will at all times protect his gluteus maximus.

He will allow nothing to penetrate his protective armor.

No matter who is really at fault, the student, and the student alone, will be made to bear the responsibility.

Basically, the "maestro" wants the student to do only what he suggests or tells him to. The less the student questions him, the more amenable this teacher will become.

Those students who are by nature subservient are quite content to study with him.

He will make no demands beyond their abilities, no ultimatums will ever be issued, and no chastisement ever rendered.

This teacher proves the point of the Peter Principle; he has, without a doubt, risen to the level of his incompetence!

His students will never measure up.

They will always be... a day late... and a dollar short!

This has always applied to any academic profession... bar none!

Fools are More to be Feared than the Wicked

"My, oh my, I do believe we may have a real Sparafucile here. Of course, you will have to learn how to broaden and darken your main voice on the low F tones in your lower register. Now we'll see whether you have the top F in your high register. I'm going to bypass your middle register and bring you up a whole octave! Ready?"

"My, oh my, oh my. What have we here? A basso with a full two octave range? Well, you certainly have just what we are looking for. What's that? You want to try going a little higher? To F sharp!"

"Well, you certainly surprised me… with an F sharp in your voice you might even be able to sing some of the bass-baritone roles."

"What, higher still? Well… I hope you know what you're doing…"

"Unbelievable! As you well know, I'm a specialist in the bass voice, but even I have never trained a basso with an A flat in his voice. You'll be sensational."

"What? You want to go higher… what's the point? Oh I see… you want to show off. Well, it's your funeral!"

"Ah, ha! I knew this would happen! You cracked on the B flat."

"Well, that proves my point. You are obviously not a tenor."

"I'm sorry to have to tell you this, but you have to know your limitations. Of course, we'll do the best we can, with what you have to work with."

(A basso with an A flat! I'll be famous!)

The Odds are Not in your Favor

Las Vegas, known the world over, owes its very existence to those unfortunates willing to risk all they may possess.

The odds of beating the house may vary, but in the long run they are formidable enough to send you to the poorhouse.

I don't like to lose, but I have a greater chance of getting my point in a crap game… than I have of finding a competent voice teacher.

The deleterious effects foisted upon students by incompetent teachers remain… for the most part… the rest of their lives.

One thing is certain: of all the students who have attempted to improve the voices they started out with, damned near all of them… have not lived long enough to do so!

Teachers

As in any profession- doctors, lawyers, Indian chiefs, etc.- voice teachers may be divided into two categories: the top 50%, and the bottom 50%.

A much sterner evaluation by the many disgruntled students I have come in contact with leads me to believe I am much too charitable.

They unanimously agree: there is indeed the top 10%, the bottom 10%, and the 80% in between... who think they know everything, but really don't know anything!

And, I daresay, there are those students who will confirm that they have hit the bottom 10%... more than once!

In face of the persistence of these factual rumors, there has to be some truth in all this.

Did I offend someone? I hear a grumbling in the background.

Diplomatic Immunity

Perhaps I'm a bit prejudiced, but, I can't help it!

During the course of my career (as a window cleaner) I have had waved under my nose every form of proof of expertise imaginable.

All of these parchments have one thing in common.

Glorified testimonials to the keen insight, the perception, and the ability of the bearer... to perform his duty!

Pardon me for laughing, but a college-issued diploma implying that any voice teacher, having passed all the various courses, is now presumably capable of teaching without inflicting severe damage... INFERS IT ONLY!

That piece of paper does not guarantee their proficiency.

I have seen more than my share of those that do not relish teaching, have no knack for communicating, and labor more for the sake of the almighty dollar than from a desire to impart whatever knowledge they may or may not possess!

And while I'm at it, may I also include those flourishing a standard bearing the title... Master of Voice?

The Bug Brigade

Now, do not believe for a moment your present teacher has always been what he presents himself to be.

"Voice teachers" drift into this method of living for a variety of reasons, far too many for me to enumerate.

Others, much more limited in scope, find no hindrance whatsoever to their teaching prowess in pursuing other options.

One teacher of repute (now under indictment) made a fortune in the "bug business."

"No bug too big, no bug too small, my method kills 'em all."

Who could resist? You made me call.

The eagerly awaited day of extermination finally arrives, and the anticipated package is deposited upon your doorstep.

Enclosed you will find a hammer, a block of wood, the necessary brochure, and... a bug.

In spite of what you may think, there is an art to all this.

Since all bugs are created unequally, (this is one of the fine points in the contract) a little finesse is required.

You just don't "slam dunk" the bug onto the block of wood... ah no, that would be unprofessional.

You gently, but firmly grasp him according to the directions enclosed, place him in the required position on the block, and then.. proceed to "whomp" him, taking care, of course, not to let your fingers get between the bug and the hammer!

Each and every week, a new bug will arrive in the mail with a detailed set of instructions.

Also included in the package (I had failed to mention this) was a summary on the art of humming.

This at times may become necessary, to discourage any suspicions on the part of the bug as to your motivations.

After your apprenticeship is over with, you too, can join the Calvinist camaraderie corps: HOBBES.

(Holy Order of the Bug Blasters Entombment Society)

Hey, there are worse ways than this to make an extra buck!

Evaluating your Ego

Just what in hell have you got to work with?

Singing demands a brutal honesty within one's self, and cannot be supported on any less rugged foundation.

Self-delusion is, by far, the one major factor that impedes progress. Inevitably, in dreaming of what he could accomplish, the student will never realize what he might have accomplished.

There is a balance in everything in the universe.

Being proud of your virtues is one thing.

There is all the difference in the world between arrogance and the awareness of one's own worth.

The gods of Vanity and Wishful Thinking dwell in harmony.

Their one implacable enemy, in common with truth, justice, honor, mom, and apple pie... is common sense!

Common sense is nothing more than a bit of logic and reasoning applied to the problem at hand.

Common sense (I've heard) is also... not all that common!

They do it "Their Way"

Alas, I must include this bit of repartee involving a few, a very few students who are quite incapable of being instructed!

This type of self-willed student (like a dog running amok), will consistently do things his own way.

Regardless of his teacher's proficiency, this animal has learned only one thing... that nobody can make him do or learn anything he does not want to!

Primarily self-taught and "born" with an amiable instrument, he will chomp at the leash, drag his ass, pretend to comply, and invariably resort to what he privately considers to be his most viable alternative.

Such a student fully intends to self-destruct in his own way!

Intelligence has nothing to do with it... it is the nature of the beast.

In their instinctive defiance of authority, they live by the rule that any rule that cannot be broken... threatens their existence!

?

The great singers of old spoke of opera not as opera but as lyric theater. That understanding has by now been almost completely lost. What do we have in its place?

Put together a modern soprano, and an interviewer for the Met. Broadcast at intermission, place between them a nice carafe of truth serum, and imagine the following appalling conversation:

Critic: Madame... in your experience as the reigning prima-donna of the Moultropolitan Opera Company, could you ever really tell what kind of a vowel any soprano is singing above an A natural?

Madame   Not really.

Critic: Doesn't it matter?

Madame   Not really.

Critic: Can you understand what they are even suggesting?

Madame   I couldn't care less. The words are incidental. The beauty of the voice is what appeals to the public.

Even if I understood the language, what difference would it make? After all, we sopranos are expected to not only sing high A's and B's... but to hold on to them!

When I have to sing a high-high C... what more could you ask for?

Please, I find Madame to be much too formal... you may address me as... your "Highness"

Love me, love my voice.

Who, amongst the peoples of the world, do you know who does not relish the sound of their own voice?

Candidates for public office obviously are the most obvious.

Even singers (believe it or not) adore the sound of their voices. (Even those that cannot sing!)

However, critical judgment must be applied.

How? Elementary, my dear Watson!

Listen to a recording of yourself. Then imagine:

The voice on this tape is not really you... and your ears are not deceiving you. This is the voice of someone you detest... perhaps even more than your mother-in-law! Your most bitter rival!

All of a sudden, everything becomes a lot clearer.

This exercise will allow you in theory to become much more objective in your summations.

Striving to become an overnight legend, you might begin to realize... that achieving greatness is one thing, but immortality... might, just might take a little bit longer.

Don't fall in love with your voice! In doing so, you will forgive it its transgressions.

The Whole Truth and Nothing But...

The truth, in itself, is noncombative.

It simply exists for those willing to seek it, and, like gold, it rewards its finder.

However, in the process, it may also demand you make some very painful changes in your way of thinking.

Naturally, you do not have to accept it.

After all, who in their right mind ever admitted to being lost?

(I may have been a little confused... but I always knew, when I was in the middle of nowhere)

The Dark Side of the Spectrum

The practice of looking the other way

Voice students have, in general, a psychological wish to sing more, and to be interrupted less.

This propensity has nothing whatsoever to do with a student's lack of devotion or dedication... but rather with his desire for peace of mind.

The student feels secure in the knowledge that since his teacher has not chided him for some infraction or other he must be doing the right thing!

Ah... not necessarily so! There well may be a deliberate malfeasance on the part of the instructor in question.

If the student is unaware of any transgressions he may be committing... don't blow the whistle... don't rock the boat!

Why create anxiety, if it can possibly be avoided?

Unless the student questions something, or is unable to continue, smooth

it over; minimize the problem; approve of the way the student himself was the one to recognize that something was not strictly kosher and, needless to say, compliment him upon his perspicacity!

Without question... such a "Maestro" is a past master of the "placebo effect"... nothing more than a glorified baby sitter!

Time marches on, and one day the student belatedly realizes that the ten

percent that was wrong with his voice in the beginning... was, in reality... ninety percent.

And he now "understands" all too well that his devoted teacher exhausted his resources... trying to perform a miracle.

That student will go to his grave never realizing that he had put his faith an trust... into the hands of a charlatan.

Those who know more than those who know nothing

Singing as an Avocation

Yes, 'tis true. As an avocation, you can sing as you please, study when you feel like it, and if a lesson might interfere in some way with more amusing plans, you are free to cancel it.

Amazingly enough, this in no way hinders you from becoming a Force to be Reckoned With.

You will continue to astound the untaught populace with your uncanny insights, profound opinions, and astute observations concerning all aspects of the musical scene.

Lordy, Lordy, Lordy!

Why pick such a venturous refuge from the real world?

Would it not have been a lot easier for you to have gone through the trials and tribulations of finger painting… whereas you could now pose as an expert on art?

Modesty "Personified"

We are all gifted to some degree.

Some among us are proficient in more than one category.

This was brought to mind by that favorite publicist's punctuation mark, the modest hyphen, which gains extraordinary potency, and increases the status of the user by a hundredfold.

Witness the recent description of a famous personality:

Artist - Poet - Conductor - Arranger - Singer - Performer -

Now this egotistical array of credits, surprisingly enough, did not also include… his obvious modesty!

Backstage, it may be common knowledge, that this humble self-taught prodigy is indeed:

Finger Painter - Plagiarist - Toe Tapper -

Music Stand Manipulator - Hog Caller - Exhibitionist.

7

Old Polish Proverb

Biding Your Time

To The Maximus

"Disorientation"

A Free Lunch

Hedging One's Bets

Laying Down the Law

Self Propulsion

Hedging His Bets

Plying His Trade

Self Preservation

Something is Missing

It Ain't Necessarily So!

The Self-Destroyers

Choir Directors

One Act at a Time

Coaching

The Ultimate Secret

Ad Nauseum

The "Magical Mystery Tour"

Old Polish Proverb

Young pigs grunt as older pigs before them grunted.

As your teacher grunts… so shall ye grunt!

In the beginning, no voice student can really make a qualified appraisal of his teacher's attributes.

Whatever qualifications your teacher may profess to possess, you may rest assured… the proof is in the pudding!

Any teacher worth his salt, should be able to demonstrate (at the very least) a good example of what he wants the student to do. (within the confines of his own tessitura)

He should also be able to describe the exact process by which he does it without recourse to subjective imagery.

Only after a period of time (years in some cases) does a student begin to realize the difference between what his teacher may advocate… and what his teacher actually does with his own voice.

Biding Your Time

In the pursuit of any endeavor close to the heart's desire, there has always been one major obstacle… no immediate compensation for the effort involved.

This is to be expected in any venture wherein the love of what you aspire to achieve must outweigh the labor involved.

The better you hope to become… the longer it takes.

Time is of the essence only to those of mercenary instincts.

Time I consider to be a small price to pay.

While it may look good in print for someone's agent to claim his client has never studied but sprang forth from the forehead of the muse, I would hope you have enough common sense to realize… that great vocal talent and a natural musical aptitude is not enough to guarantee success.

Damned near every voice student I've ever encountered, has had, in his own humble opinion, these very virtues!

Don't fool yourself! Every new songbird springing up "overnight" like a shiny new dime… has spent at least five to ten years achieving this "overnight" success.

To the Maximus

Unless the student is comatose, dead drunk, or otherwise incapacitated, the voice teacher's Prime Directive, first and foremost, is to bring the student's voice to the "Maximus"

No "pussyfooting" allowed!

The neophyte student must be made to understand that this procedure is to his advantage.

This means only that, for a few moments at least, the teacher shall bring forth in every lesson whatever the student's instrument is capable of at that time... and beyond!

The student should be aware of the fact that his instrument is being "boosted", temporarily, to its "outer limits"... somewhat correctly, I hope.

Neither the teacher nor the student owes the other an apology, if the results are less than soul-satisfying.

In this way, the instrument (along with the ears of the afflicted) soon

learns to contend with the sometimes disagreeable demands made upon it.

"Disorientation"

Immediately after a vocal "change", wherein the instrument has now formed within itself a new identity, the student will inevitably find his "voice" sounds strange to him.

His voice has now become a trifle smoother, mellower, and much easier to project.

However, his hearing and his senses will betray him.

Unaccustomed to these strange new sensations, he will be quite certain the voice has become weaker, less resonant, and horror of horrors... he is losing it!

Au contraire, not so!

The student's voice has entered a new stage of perfection.

The instrument is not "out of whack"... he singer is!

In the early stages of the game, unless the teacher recognizes exactly what has transpired, and why, the bewildered student may beg forgiveness for imagined sins, contribute his possessions to the poor, and fervently promise to mend his ways.

A Free Lunch

In the academic profession some professors have the integrity to live with the consequences of their ideas. More power to them.

However, while the unbelievable arrogance and incompetence rampant in the vocal "arts" field has led to the ruin of many a promising voice, no failure of a voice student has ever forced a teacher to give up his or her "profession"

Why should they?

The voice is so subjective a subject, and even talented students so credulous and eager to believe any "expert", and the part played by good training so little credited, let alone understood, that even those teachers aware of the consequences of their ideas, and the havoc they perpetrated... were never forced to pay for them!

The same principle applies when you bring your car in for a tune-up. You don't know anything about garage procedures or what is required, so naturally you trust the mechanic to do the best he can with the junk heap you've brought in. After the mechanic has changed the oil, added a little anti-freeze, kicked your tires and cleaned your windshield, he will present you with the bill.

Upon parting, he will of course remind you that he did the best he could with what you're driving, but you really should trade it in!

Hedging One's Bets

This philosophy is espoused by your doctor.

Your doctor of course has no desire to overly upset you, but he does paint a rather bleak picture of your symptoms.

He will of course do everything in his power to tide you over before rigor mortis sets in.

In common with those voice teachers who manage to both promise the moon and promise nothing at the same time, this doctor has learned the hard way.

If he is overly optimistic about your chances,- the operation really isn't that difficult; the boil does appear to be in remission; all the signs are right; he had even brought his lucky rabbit's foot - and you still drop dead... he won't look too good!

Dare I presume your doctor has passed his postgraduate course in frog dissection?

Laying Down the Law

That old navy term "shape up or ship out", means exactly what it says… dereliction of duty is reason for discharge.

In any academic institution devoted to higher learning, many a fine teacher would like nothing better… than to kick ass once in a while with a dense or incorrigible student as target, with the secret hope, said student would be drafted into the "Foreign Legion", and in the process… learn a little discipline!

Of course, this fundamental breach of etiquette directed at a student's breeches would arouse the ire of the school administration.

After all, students form the basis of their bread and butter.

Imagine the chaos that would ensue, if I had been teaching in a conservatory on the day I felt impelled to cry out, in the course of a buttoned-up soprano's lesson, "Put your pussy into it!"

Now… the soprano immediately understood what was lacking… in her performance of "Musetta's Waltz Song."

There are those who firmly believe the end justifies the means, and those that do not.

As far as I'm concerned… any which way I can!

Self Propulsion

A baritone I once knew, forced to scrabble for those minor roles that posed no great challenge to his voice or musicianship, told me he knew when to quit.

In the formative years of slogging through the muck and mire, climbing mountains, hurdling crevices, weathering the elements, every student will, ultimately, find himself facing the mighty ocean.

Now what…?

His self-propulsion will now carry him one small step further.

Undaunted, he puts on his galoshes and will now proceed to walk on water!

I don't care what you may aspire to; the bottom line in any endeavor is to have the fortitude to persevere!

No Guts, No Glory!

Hedging his Bets

In evaluating a student's vocal apparatus, the margin for error is more or less 100 per cent.

I imagine the prospective student would naturally wish to know exactly what he has to work with... no ifs, ands, or buts.

It does not take a great deal of intelligence to realize... that a student having a somewhat agreeable and easy access to a note or two above the staff... must be a tenor!

That was the easy part... but his teacher knows by instinct, he still has a very sticky situation here.

The tenor in question "tops out" at B flat.

Now the "Maestro" knows enough to let the B flat alone... if it ain't broke... don't fix it! He will then attempt to teach the student whatever else he deems necessary... studiously avoiding giving him anything to sing... above a B flat!

Four years later (more or less) the student now armed with a certificate endorsing his proficiency ventures forth into the real world. All is not quite what he had imagined it to be.

Now faced with reality, his survival instincts take over.

Henceforth, he will proclaim to one and all, that his voice is a rare gift indeed... a truly astonishing "B flat baritone"!

Plying His Trade

Another high ranking official, caught with his hands in the public till, protested his innocence, castigated those casting aspersions upon his integrity, and proclaimed to all his unique accomplishments in his chosen field.

Even after having been exposed as the charlatan he is, this snaked-tongued charmer will continue to ply his trade!

(The only thing he would not steal was a red hot stove)

I would sooner trust a public official than a voice teacher. Or even a used car salesman. At least, after having bought a used car, you will find out almost immediately what is not right with it... regardless of the salesman's protestations to the contrary.

With a voice teacher... it often takes years.

Self Preservation

During my salad years, there flourished this one "maestro" (of the old school) who inexplicably managed to garner students to his threshold.

One of these students, having been nurtured by the maestro for several years, suddenly became aware that he was losing whatever voice he had to begin with!

He expressed his fears to his mentor.

The "maestro", reluctant as ever to lose a student, and being of a kind and genteel nature, now realized he had no choice!

He promptly proceeded to throw said student out of his studio... in order to forestall any further damage to his own reputation.

Something is Missing

Those very few voice teachers that can demonstrate to their pupils exactly what is required, and why, are (in my opinion) rare enough to be considered... an endangered species.

Every student I have ever spoken to, has acknowledged knowing, or hearing of, teachers that professed to understand the intricate workings of the vocal mechanism in spite of the fact that they themselves could not sing!

This is indeed a paradox!

I don't doubt for a moment the existence of conductors, coaches, and chorus directors who possess an immaculate ear and no doubt know their trade, but even those few who have actually studied singing for a while are in no way qualified to teach voice!

Would you want to take flying lessons from someone who has only traveled as a passenger?

As I have said, even those performers who are quite accomplished in the art of singing often know little or nothing about how they do what they do.

Consider for a moment the immaculate Count Dracula. He puzzles me. Known the world over for his fastidious attire and impeccable grooming... since he cannot see himself in the mirror... how does he do it?

Aye! Verily... something is missing!

It Ain't Necessarily So!

Sopranos seek out sopranos, baritones seek baritones, and tenors are convinced only another tenor can rectify their vocal ailments.

It is only natural that a student might feel more compatible with a teacher of his or her own sex and vocal type.

This deep-rooted bias really works against the beginning student.

The student will attempt to emulate his teacher's sound and identify with his teacher's assessment of what that particular vocal category consists of. Thus, every fault in the teacher's apparatus or vocal technique (no teacher is perfect) will then be passed on to the student.

This is not the best of all possible worlds!

I myself had studied with a soprano who not only reined in my "wild

horse" instincts and calmed my macho tendency to let my voice run amok, but also persuaded me to give at least "lip service" to repertoire I balked at. I was the better for it.

All things considered, femininity is a wonderful virtue.

But in retrospect, this also I can attest to... half the female students I've ever known needed a more masculine approach, in order to survive.

(To put it delicately... a good kick in the ass!)

The Self-Destroyers

In the middle of the prairie a lone sycamore stood. Everyone for miles around knew that tree was there. For some reason or other, this plaintive waif of the prairie was denied the companionship usually associated with its species.

Being the only tree in this barren land... the inevitable occurred.

Coming in for a landing, the pilot of a malfunctioning aircraft reasonably assume the only proper place to land ...was in the tree!

Now there's a singleminded sense of purpose!

It reminds me of this one tenor's fixation on learning how to control his "vibrato", so as to-presumably-control his "tone"

This tenor (without a doubt) is also the one who taught his parrot to say... "Here, Kitty, Kitty"!

Choir Directors

During my student days I was "drafted" into volunteering for a local church choir.

The choir director's credentials were immaculate; not only could he transpose on sight, he also knew the church literature, was a consummate musician, and had accompanied, as a pianist, a world famous singer on tour.

I soon found out he was true to his calling. He couldn't sing his way out of a paper bag, knew nothing whatsoever about the vocal instrument and actually held in contempt all singers in general!

Far-fetched? No Sir! Par for the course. In my own experience, and that of my students, it seems to be universal.

I do not doubt there are choir directors out there well versed in their craft, and it is, indeed, a noble calling. But, choir directing (to me) seems almost to be a refuge for those involved.

As to the choir members... if 'tis true that the meek will inherit the earth, they will be the first in line.

As to how those few (very few) valiant ones who have stood up to make their feelings known, they have learned the hard way.

As far as the pastor is concerned, he knows his priorities. He will always side WITH the director and AGAINST any choral member grumbling about something or other.

P.S. If for any reason the choir director drops dead, don't harbor any

illusions about the next one!

One Act At A Time

You wish to learn a role? Fine. It will at least give you a sense of accomplishment and a taste of in-depth study.

However, I would suggest you do not spend all that time and energy learning something that may take years for you to implement.

Murphy's Law dictates...no role ever comes by that you have already memorized!

Therefore, select any half-dozen roles you would ordinarily investigate, and proceed to learn just the first act of each.

This is far better for your instrument because of the variety of styles and languages encountered.

Coaching

Inevitably, the day will come, when the student feels secure enough to seek out the services of a coach.

Don't think for a moment that an accompanist (even a good one) can adequately fulfill your needs.

Good coaches, presumably well versed in the accepted traditions of the bel canto repertoire, are becoming rarer and rarer.

A coach's business is to teach the student to deliver what the composer intended, and why, as far as the musical, interpretive, and stage values are concerned; tempered by a tacit understanding of each pupil's individual vocal assets and limitations.

All in all, a formidable process!

Doing his or her duty, a coach cannot help but acquire a fragmentary knowledge of the singing process and has often been able to pave the way for the impoverished student to better understand his vocal mechanism.

The Ultimate Secret

The big dog in the neighborhood digs a deep hole in the ground, proceeds to cover it over, and thereafter stands guard over it.

All the other dogs in the neighborhood just know he must have the biggest, juiciest bone ever!

However, try as they may, they never quite succeed in unearthing the big dog's treasure, and so acknowledge among themselves (a lot of commiseration here) that he possesses a treasure indeed!

I have met more singers than anyone would wish to meet, who profess a knowledge of that one ultimate secret, enabling them to sing as well as they do.

Each and every one of them steadfastly refuses to part with it. And why should they!

Remember the fable about the emperor's new clothes? Well, the big dog has nothing whatsoever buried in that hole!

Ad Nauseum

The soprano had a tough choice to make. Which of her two arias should she sing for her audition?

She decided upon "Vissi D'arte."

For this I was grateful; I didn't have to suffer through another "Un Bel Di."

What this soprano and the countless others out there do not understand (or refuse to acknowledge), is that they were ALL born with the capacity to sing the coloratura repertoire.

This includes ALL the female voices.

The female instrument is a far more resilient and adaptable organ than it is commonly understood to be by either teachers or students.

Coloratura is nothing more than an ornamental style, which, by its very nature, contributes greatly to instilling within the voice the necessary patterns of technique absolutely mandatory in freeing up a recalcitrant instrument.

As far as I'm concerned, from the very first lesson onward, ALL female voices should begin vocal training with the simplest and the most easily understood coloratura arias written for their specific voice type.

I should mention there exists a minor drawback to all this.

You cannot "coast" in coloratura. Both the student and the teacher…

are now going to have to work their asses off!

No pain… no gain!

The "Magical Mystery Tour"

All Aboard

Picking a voice teacher is the same as getting on a bus, hoping the bus will drop you off at your destination.

Regardless of whatever source may have informed you that this bus does indeed go where you want, trust no one else's sense of direction absolutely… unless the signposts you pass on the way (we are speaking of your own, indisputable vocal progress here) tell you the bus is indeed en route and drawing ever closer to the goals you wish to achieve, the destination the sign on the bus has promised.

A lot of those who have traveled on the bel canto bus for years …still have no idea of where the hell they are!

8

Beyond the Studio - Auditions and Other Tortures

Limurictus

Auditioning

The Arena

Against All Odds

Beware the "Qualified Authority"

We Who Gather Together

The Malignant Mouth

"Phobias"

"Bluff"

You Find the Gold and I'll Split it With You

     Fifty - Fifty

Was That You?

The Mandibular Menace

The Ingratitude of it All

Honesty

My Dictum

Practice

Limerictus

Abbasso Capriccioso

Achille Belmondo, a basso rotondo
incensed o'er his billing secondo
ate the stage in a rage
and the score page by page
then burped all his tones in profundo!

Auditioning

I assume you brought your music?

I remember well the times I have auditioned. I can count on the fingers of one hand the few times I received a smile of encouragement and perhaps a word or two to put me at ease.

These occasions were the exceptions!

Most auditions seem to be asking… "If you are so God-damn good why are you auditioning?"

For the most part, I was treated with disdain, by these artsy- craftsy bastards, before I had even begun to sing!

P.S. Don't expect any help from the piano player.

Most are quite competent, but… they couldn't care less.

The Arena

Harbor no illusions to the contrary… you are going into combat!

It well may be the closest thing to High Noon you will ever encounter. You stand alone. No one to hold your hand, back you up or give encouragement.

And this is as it should be.

Countless aspirants have expired in this selective arena, never to venture forth again. Even those blessed by Mother Nature with more than their share

of talent have fallen by the wayside.

An audition is more than a test of your ability as a performer.

It is also a crucible, wherein the fire that tempers steel… also melts wax mannequins!

Against All Odds

You must presume beyond a shadow of a doubt that you, and you alone, have what they need.

Whether the "powers that be" realize this or not is another story.

All's fair in love, war, and auditions, regardless of the outcome.

You must consider whatever occurs at each audition as part of the force of destiny… not putting you down or pushing you back, but leading you onward and upward, to that unreachable star, almost, but not quite, within your grasp.

Beware the "Qualified Authority"

In the struggle for supremacy, many a gifted soul has fallen by the wayside. Par for the course!

Needless to say, there are those singers who have taken the initiative in their ceaseless struggle to prove themselves.

Setting forth on their own (no grants, scholarships, or even unemployment insurance to sustain them) they will inevitably collide with the "Eminent Authorities"

Now, to the point.

Whether or not you may have auditioned brilliantly, matters not.

Far more than your vested interests are at stake.

The auditioners' are, too!

You must understand; they hear only what they want to hear!

You cannot fault them for adhering to their viewpoint, no matter how biased and mean spirited it may seem to be.

These authorities in question: voice teachers, conductors, directors, underlings, ad nauseum, are in essence "protecting their turf"… or their asses… as the case may be.

But, take heart… half the singers rejected out of hand, for whatever reasons you may conjure up, have soldiered on to take their rightful niche in the scheme of things.

The bottom line… you must become better than you dared hope!

P.S. And whether you realize it or not.. you too may be destined to officiate in the future… as a "Qualified Authority"

We Who Gather Together

Lo! The Poor Chorister, the backbone of the opera house.

They sweat their asses off and are often maligned.

The Powers that Be often consider them a necessary evil.

The Impresarios of the smaller companies almost treat them with disdain.

The chorister can make more money off his paper route than the pittance (if any) offered for his singing.

Even the Chorus Masters (many of whom cannot sing at all) consider

choristers to be but a step above the stagehands.

Then along comes this ass, the tenor soloist. Born with a "Silver Spoon" in his throat, he now proceeds to hold court.

Well, he is what the public pays for!

But choristers, (being a rather resilient bunch, and not readily discouraged) manage one way or another to transcend the slings and arrows of their rocky profession, and to soldier on… and… some do indeed become Forces to Be Reckoned With.

The Malignant Mouth

As in all professions, in singing you will inevitably encounter someone who will proceed to tear you apart.

If the diatribe is meant only to benefit your working knowledge and you sense no malice involved, Thou Shalt Listen!

On the other hand, (we assume you have first seriously considered its

possible validity) you may feel this attack upon your vocal and musical persona to be spiteful in nature, contributing nothing whatsoever to your fund of knowledge.

Were you to have suffered a vocal miscarriage, cracked on all your high notes, started salivating, or been booed off the stage, the frustration factor of this baneful backbiter would have been alleviated and there would have been no

reason to verbally vilify you.

Do not react emotionally… all you do is add fuel to the fire.

Of course there is nothing in the rule books (lawyers excepted) that says you cannot ask this miscreant to step outside, and then proceed to teach him manners… in an "uncivilized manner"!

"Phobias"

While cleaning the windows on the top floor of a downtown building I paused in my labors to light up a cigarette.

Almost immediately a young woman stormed over and demanded I cease and desist, threatening dire consequences!

[Aghast at a Social Blunder of Unprecedented Proportions]

Regardless of the fact that the window was open and her work station well over 50 feet away, she was adamant. With a shrug of my shoulders... I acknowledged her self-righteous phobia.

Anyone serving in the performing arts field will have a phobia or two to accommodate them. Why not? They have more of a right than anybody. Some phobias can even be considered "user friendly"!

Ah, but when they interfere... an irrational fear can inhibit the persona to such an extent, it becomes a destructive force.

The singer must learn to recognize and dispel all such fears; both real and imaginary, as they arrive upon the scene.

Thou Shalt Rid Thyself of Thy Phobias... or you will carry them to your vocal grave.

"Bluff"

All singers bluff... it goes with the territory.

Every singer, I don't care who, or how famous, will bluff.

Even with the best intentions in the world, every singer caught up in a discussion of the vocal arts at some time or other has had to resort to saving face.

Rather than admit to a lack of knowledge on his part, he will desperately strive to piece together whatever he may know, to stay abreast of, or, in desperation, fend off the subject at hand.

No malice is implied here... only that a goodly portion of any profession is riddled with insecurities, and opera singing... more so!

(I don't deny I've "bluffed" more than my share... but my reasons were obviously-better than anyone else's!)

You Find the Gold and I'll Split It With You...Fifty-Fifty

Through no fault of his own, every singer fortunate enough to have made his mark will also acquire a host of former acquaintances scrambling for the recognition they so richly deserve.

Each and every one of them will now piously affirm that without their divine intervention his musical and vocal shortcomings would have been

impossible to overcome!

Even those that had denigrated his talents... now clasp him to their bosom.

And why shouldn't they?

After all, it is in their own best interests.

Of course, any singer daring to confront these parasites and perhaps contradict their viewpoint would immediately be branded as an ungrateful wretch and not worthy of their consideration.

It has always been and it always will be.

Was That You?

Many years ago, the late, great movie tenor Mario Lanza auditioned for this one opera company by mailing in a recording of that tenor staple, "Celeste Aida."

The Powers That Were liked what they heard and immediately summoned him for a live audition. They were not only impressed, but allowed as how he was much better in person than on his recording.

A few years later (being prudent) Mario belatedly confessed he was not the tenor on the recording.

Well, that should hardly matter; after all, by that time the Powers That Were couldn't have cared less and why should they?

Nary a one of them had recognized the voice on the recording to be that of the immortal tenor... Enrico Caruso!

It happens all the time; "Was that you, was that you?"

The Mandibular Menace

One budding soprano, on the verge of a glorious career, abruptly withdrew from the concert scene. "Never again", she vowed, would she venture upon

the stage.

There may be differing accounts of what transpired that evening, but, in essence, it seems that during the climactic moments of her debut, an alligator had wandered onstage, and promptly proceeded to bite… her most prominent protuberance!

She thereupon declared she would never return, until that infamous creature had been disposed of.

For all I know, that alligator may have been a music lover.

(It could happen!)

The Ingratitude of it All

A noted soprano, returning in triumph from her final concert tour, encountered one of her most ardent admirers.

After the amenities were over, this adoring fan questioned her concerning the lucky charm he had lent her.

She replied that the charm in question (a lovely gold brooch) had indeed stood her in good stead, and thanked him profusely… however, as to its

whereabouts, she hadn't the foggiest!

In the confusion of returning from abroad, she must have misplaced it somewhere, but one of these days, she will get around to finding it!

Years go by…

Rest assured, pangs of conscience or a vague sense of commitment are rare in the creative arts field, and this shameless soprano's baser instincts.. will never allow her to give up her deceitful decorum and give in to gratitude!

Harbor no illusions, either, as to the humanitarian instincts of management, impresarios, agents, etc… their "vested interests" predominate.

The bottom line may well be… whom can you rely upon, to venture forth on a dark and stormy night, with cash in hand… to bail you out of the local constabulary?

Honesty

A truism among singers generally agreed upon: a singer may have impeccable judgment pertaining to another performer's abilities, but alas, he is quite incapable of judging himself!

This is not as it should be. Every singer must of necessity be his own critic.

He must be able to determine precisely what he is doing.

Honesty (that often maligned term) must be his co-conspirator.

My Dictum

March or die

Private:	"Sergeant, I have an ingrown toenail!"
Sergeant:	"Good! That will help you march tomorrow."
Private:	"Did I mention I also had a sprained wrist?"
Sergeant:	"Oh My! You will still march tomorrow, but you will not have to salute me."
Private:	"It also occurs to me, that I had neglected to bring my crutches."
Sergeant:	"You lucked out! I shall see to it that you will only have to complete the obstacle course!"

Practice

The errors a voice student or any performer commits in practice, issue forth in rehearsal.

All mistakes of a technical or musical nature committed in rehearsal… ultimately issue forth in performance.

Although the prompter can aid and abet a performer suffering a sudden memory lapse, you will need divine intervention (which is seldom forth coming… and for good reason) to subsidize shoddy musicianship, faulty technique, and a wretched retention.

You cannot correct anything at the last minute!

The subconscious habit patterns and reflexes of a lifetime will consistently outwit you.

9

A Surplus of Tonnage

Scholarships

Turn Up the Volume

Listening

The Indelicacy of it All

Woof, Woof

The Last Round-Up

Self-Induced Melancholia

The Injustice of it All

Pompous Prose

Thanks... For the Memory

"Tenoritis"

The Raven, the Magpie, and the Mocking Bird

Too Much... Too Soon

"Animation"

Poor Rambo

Link Trainer

Poise

Where Angels Fear to Tread

Your Better Half

A Surplus of Tonnage

Sopranos (it seems to me) have the most difficult path to follow.

Opportunities to perform before the public are most certainly not as prevalent as they used to be.

In order to make your mark, you must face innumerable obstacles, some of which will be above and beyond your control or expertise.

Almost seeming to personify the law of gravity, the sopranos of yesteryear were indeed... a hefty bunch!

Time marches on, and this is no longer true.

You can look like hell if you sing like heaven in the opera house, but, in the age of televised opera, your public is going to be a helluva lot more critical of the package, whatever the contents may be.

With the competition as fierce as it is, if you still "fit" into this category, (look in the mirror if you have to) why penalize yourself?

Contrary to the edicts of old, a surplus of tonnage does not protect the voice in any way!

The floorboards backstage have more than their share of burdens to bear.

P.S. I've heard rumors now and then, of certain sopranos, who very suspiciously sounded like they were "mooing" on the high notes!

Scholarships

These Dream Boats are sailing around out there, all right! The promises of a sweet voyage, upon the waters of infinite patience and wisdom, bestowed upon you in recognition of your more sterling qualities... are few and far between.

In order for you to fulfill your rightful place in the scheme of things, you should realize... these competitions are tough enough... to scare the pants off a gorilla!

I have no intention of dissuading you from entering any of them.

The pressures encountered will fortify you.

This final thought... most "scholarships" promise a hell of a lot more than they deliver!... Some restrictions may apply.

Turn up the Volume

Once upon a time, many long years ago, I can still remember when damn near every aspiring performer who chose to tread the boards had to be heard au natural... without amplification!

Show Business in those days still had some integrity.

The electronic amplification process has launched more careers in the last half of this century than all the generations before it.

There is no longer the need for anyone having to learn the tools of his trade.

What had been a source of pride... the acoustic voice... has now been prostituted to the snap, crackle, pop, and static of the boom-boxes.

The mouse that roared can now mumble to his heart's content.

The legitimate theatre has become vocally illiterate.

What I'm hearing is the sizzle... not the steak.

Now the inevitable question arises. Will management now reassure me (with a money-back guarantee) that what I paid to see and hear, is truly what I came to see and hear... and not a prerecording...?

Is nothing sacred?

Listening

In any rehearsal of a workshop production, the cast will usually include someone showing only a cursory interest in the proceedings.

Whether through harboring a thinly disguised contempt for the other participants or through sheer ignorance, this "artist" is simply not interested in listening to others. He has his own ax to grind.

Impatiently "killing time" while awaiting his turn to sing, as far as he is concerned... the other singers may as well be on the moon.

Maria Callas had the reputation of knowing everyone's part.

(Perhaps even better than those involved.)

This diva understood that listening to others is not external; It is internal!

In other words, it is not extraneous... it is essential!

The Indelicacy of it All

Singers very often just cannot cope with a negative critique of any sort. Even the best-intended and most intelligent comment offends.

This becomes much more apparent after the performer has reached a stage of proficiency… to almost earn a living. Although some may appear to be somewhat indifferent to your remarks you damn well know you are being viewed with a "jaundiced eyeball"

"It works for me" is a reply that does not encourage any outside interference with another singer's technique.

Perhaps, in time, they might acknowledge that you did indeed have a valid point of view, but… "In God's name, why weren't you more delicate in your approach?"

Fragile egos here.

I do not care where the comment originates. If I am informed my bumper has just fallen off my car, I will investigate!

I will prove to my own satisfaction, whether the bumper is there, merely loose, or has, indeed, fallen off!

Woof, Woof

An actual police report was filed by an irate female over a conflict involving her peach trees.

She had hired a man to pick these peaches off her trees. Hours later, when he had finished the job, she became incensed to find… he was eating one!

Tempers often flare, before, during, and after a rehearsal.

You may indeed be the reigning prima donna of the opera company, but consider for a moment…

The conductor doesn't really know the music, the bassoonist has a "fat lip", the orchestra personnel are grumbling about the heat being turned off, and the choristers are snuffling up a storm.

Keep your "cool" 'Tis better to be remembered as an amiable colleague, than to be referred to as the one who likes dog biscuits.

The Last Round-Up

Church singers (in general) seem almost to have a lackadaisical interest in the proceedings. This may be due in part to the repetitive series of scales, words, and melodic intervals they are made to sing... or just plain boredom.

Their one crushing contribution to the congregation, above and beyond their volume, tonal quality, or musicianship, is, you guessed it... their talent for "rendering" the words.

The choir director's principal concern is with the music..period. Fine!

That's what he's there for!

But in order to achieve the quality of tone he considers to be "harmonious" within this group, his magic word is "Blend" Under his tutelage... Thou shalt blend thy voice with thy neighbors'!

Since no one is permitted to express their own individuality, they will soon become, in essence, members of the herd!

Herding his charges along in this manner, each and every member of this chorale will end up as a buffalo chip!

No vocal instrument can survive this sort of abuse, and, for the sake of whatever you may have left to work with... you damn well better believe it!

Stifling your voice in this manner negates the spontaneity, the life force so essential to its health and welfare.

Any message to be delivered... falls by the wayside.

Peas annd da Erth... Gud weel too Awel... Onely da Trooth Hertz.

Self-Induced Melancholia

This occurs most frequently among the higher strung. However, everyone succumbs. Sooner or later, disaster strikes.

It is... inevitable.

I recall the sad tale of the woebegone debutante.

After the ball was over, she was inconsolable. In her heart, she just knew she had been the ugliest girl there!

No amount of commiseration could quell her miseria.

That she had been the only female there... made no difference at all!

The Injustice of it All

Each and every performer has undergone the traumatic experience of a less than favorable review.

The entire history of music abounds with personal prejudices, vainglorious viewpoints, immaculate misconceptions, and ultimately... the pernicious "poison pen" profiteers.

Fair or foul, it matters not... why should you be an exception?

Learn to roll with the punches!

Wrap yourself in the warm blanket of your supporters.

This will shield you from the icy breath of the miscreants who dare to view you with disdain.

Now I must assume you can tell the difference between an honest admirer... and a fawning flatterer.

Aye! There's the rub. Just because your mother loves your voice... does not mean the cat wishes to endure it!

P.S. Perhaps I should recant that last remark; I do not wish to incur the wrath of more homeless kitties than necessary!

Pompous Prose

An opinion is only a collage of emotional impressions bundled together to form a particular viewpoint. Regardless of the pros and cons of the matter, to be "opinionated" commits you to a viewpoint that will brook no opposition.

In politics, religion, and the arts this is readily apparent.

What I abhor is the self obstinacy of those that consider their printed opinions "deathless prose"... etched in stone!

In the arts, anyway, there is nothing wrong with a perception based on gut instinct, whereas a knowledge of the issues involved may be inconsequential.

The old adage, "believe half of what you see and nothing of what you hear" ... still holds water.

I can't remember the last time I read a review wherein any two or three of the reviewers unanimously agreed with each other!

All you can do is read between the lines!

Thanks... for the Memory

Now singing, as some have declared, may indeed be 90 % memory, but since most singers are not gifted with total recall... they must "sweat out" this learning process.

The more you memorize (correctly I hope) the more adept your mind becomes at retaining what you must know.

While it is entirely possible to pick up what you need to know by ear or by rote, (some blind singers have done remarkably well) this poses only one drawback... you learn the mistakes too!

Aside from the conductor, the second hardest working member of any company during a performance is (think about it)... the prompter.

Unheralded and unacclaimed, his job is exactly what it implies; to give aid and comfort to the cast... even, at times, to possess a remarkable ability to sense a performer's impending distress.

At point blank range, he always manages to cue his targets.

Do I dare hope... you understand what he uses for ammunition?

Now, of course, if all the singers of an opera company did have total recall, management would then save itself a bundle, and during intermission... relegate the prompter to assist the patrons at the bar to either drown or resurrect their memories.

"Tenoritis"

Tenoritis - an affliction of the male ego for which there is... no known cure. All in all... the ultimate male ego.

A tenor with this disease creates havoc among his colleagues.

After all, Divine Right has its privileges!

This most singular of all heirs apparent to the throne will always disavow (most of the time anyhow) any identification with the Deity - preferring to be known only as... His understudy.

As far as the choristers (the workaholics of any opera company) are concerned, most tenors are "slightly stupid."

Don't take anyone's intelligence for granted... even your own!

The Raven, the Magpie, and the Mocking Bird

The raven, the magpie, and the mocking bird, having nothing better to do at the moment, were bickering amongst themselves as to who had the better singing voice and vocal technique. Each in turn criticized the others unmercifully for some fault or breach of the bel canto process.

This squabble came to an abrupt halt, however, when the sublime song of a nightingale was heard in the distance. Each bird, in his own way... recognized a common foe.

They then proceeded to join forces, and cast unprecedented aspersions upon this itinerant intruder who had the temerity to challenge their dominance.

Don't pity the poor nightingale.

She understands all too well... it goes with the territory!

Too Much...Too Soon

The man with the big cigar stared in shocked disbelief.

"Son, I've booked acts from here to Cucamonga, and even beyond.

I've heard rumors, but what you're telling me is impossible, I can't buy it, nobody can be that good. I mean... six girls in a row?"

The young man (with the assistance of the impresario's nubile secretary) proceeded to demonstrate.

The next evening, the "Greatest Lover in the World" entered the theatre accompanied by a bevy of beauties.

After much fanfare and a rather tumultuous reception, it soon became apparent, however, that something was amiss. Striving valiantly, he almost succeeded, but alas, t'was not to be... the third in line (along with the audience) was left... unsatisfied.

Backstage, after his inept performance, the impresario was inconsolable. "I don't understand, how could you do this to me? In all the years I've been in business, never, I say never, have I been so humiliated, Oy Vey!"

The young man nodded in agreement. He too, was mortified.

"I don't understand either... everything went fine in rehearsal!"

Conserve your Resources.

"Animation"

History records the inept performer who adhered to the hoary dictum "Don't move on stage."

Pursuing an abysmal career in the theatre, reduced to portraying grotesque aliens, supine corpses, occasional furniture and even (heaven forbid) appearing on T.V. talk shows, he was asked why he didn't quit.

Undeterred in the slightest, he naturally replied…

"What! and give up show business?"

Regardless of the beauty of the voice, the interpretive nuances, the musicality of the performer, etc., one can become quite exasperated at the inability of a performer to move on stage.

Possessing an innate fear of appearing or feeling ridiculous, said performer will now take root, sprout branches, wait to be watered… and play "safe"

Perhaps this performer had seen a bronzed placard hanging in a world famous opera house foyer:

> On This Stage During a Performance of Rigoletto
>
> The Baritone Signor Bottiglia… Alienated The Entire Audience

My viewpoint… no singer really has to "act"… just react!

Give me some form of animation… preferably ambulatory.

Poor Rambo

All singers will periodically suffer from self-induced fits of depression concerning their vocal indispositions. Whether 'tis real or imagined, makes no never mind. It is actually a form of self pity, and will in time alleviate itself.

Regardless of its origin, I equate this form of melancholic behavior with Rambo's Last Stand.

Bleeding from a dozen wounds, he shrugs them off as inconsequential.

Again, and again, he endeavors to hurl himself into the fray... only to withdraw at the last moment.

A man can only take so much, and even Rambo... must concede.

After all, an ingrown toenail... is not to be trifled with!

Link Trainer

During W.W.2, all pilots underwent navigational instruction.

Under an enclosed hood the fledgling flyers learned how to fly, navigate, deliver their ordnance and fulfill their missions.

Learning the hard way (in actual combat) would obviously result in an unprecedented number of casualties, so this apprenticeship program was initiated.

Now, as good as they may have been in the classroom, only the experience of flying a genuine mission could hone their survival skills. Every bird in the wild has had to learn this lesson.

Moral? Thou shalt perform! If you wait until you are ready... you will never be ready!

Poise

Poise is a manner of achieving control in a difficult situation. It can be acquired... but for many people, only after years of intense self-discipline.

Poise enables you to sell yourself to the audience, giving them at least the impression of complete control and mastery of your art.

The conceit that impels a performer to attempt something above and beyond his limited mastery of the skills required (nothing unusual about this) may be forgiven... if the performer's personality or general savoir-faire... transcends his obvious lack of vocal expertise.

Where Angels Fear to Tread

Any ambassador serving the interests of the United States has always been considered to have a cushy job.

As in any profession, there are those (albeit a very few) who will take it upon themselves to try to straighten things out.

Regardless of their proficiency, these men of principle have been reviled, and their persons defamed, for daring to criticize the host country's aims and endeavors.

C`est la Vie!

You may well find the same reaction, when you feel compelled to tell someone what you humbly believe to be the truth.

The party in question does not want to hear, or even tolerate, any viewpoint contrary to its own!

[Outraged Indignation at the Audacity of a Lower Life Form]

"Only God can criticise me... who the hell do you think you are?"

Who do I have to be... His next of kin?

Your Better Half

Domestic tranquillity... is not all that tranquil.

If your domestic partner is not fully aware of your ambition, and the lengths you will go to achieve it... the storm clouds gather.

Your partner has really fallen in love with the glamour of it all... but the better, or non artistic, half of an artistic marriage (being of a practical nature as far as results are concerned) takes a dim view when nothing appears on the immediate horizon.

They quickly become disillusioned, and understand only... that it took you twice as long to become half as good as you thought you were going to be!

Therefore, thou shalt be obligated to find a practical job, quit spending time and money on an intangible dream, get down to earth... and put out the garbage!

P.S. I've been through it...

10

The Lottery

"Charisma"

Great Rejoicing in the House of Tenors

What Have I Got to Lose?

"Sympathy Pains"

User-Friendly

Compliments

Stammering

The Power of Imagination

Nobodys Perfect

Verbal Contracts

Bundle it Up

Better Luck Next Time

Supertitles

"With A Little Bit O'Luck"

The Lottery

Achieving fame and fortune in a singing career is akin to winning the lottery. Needless to say, once you succeed, you will then be accosted by those that feel you may be able to "open doors" for them.

The local hooker (plying her trade) was approached by a potential customer inquiring as to her availability.

Sizing him up, (no pun intended) she asked him if he was married. Upon receiving an affirmative reply, she then demonstrated her own brand of integrity.

"You will have to seek elsewhere, I am only for the needy... not for the greedy!"

Let your conscience be your guide.

"Charisma"

Many a critic has complained... "It's not that I liked the voice that much... it's just that I did not object to it!"

In an aural sense, we all perceive differently. One man's meat is another man's poison. No rhyme or reason is necessary. Since no voice is to every listener's taste, and many a once-loved voice does indeed wear out its welcome, a performer's charisma must often put across what his instrument is not capable of achieving.

Any which way you define it... call it charm, appeal, magnetism, etc.: in the subconscious appraisal of any performance, the perception of "charisma" often determines far more than the ear alone.

Great Rejoicing in the House of Tenors.

One of their more gifted colleagues had "lost" his voice!

No longer able to sustain anything above the staff, he was now forced to retire from the scene.

The crocodile tears now shed for him... could have floated the Queen Mary.

The remaining tenors closed ranks against all newcomers, and, the field thus narrowed each set forth to become the old star's successor.

In any field of endeavor, this is inevitable. You, too... shall pass...

What Have I Got to Lose!

The vocal instrument, in spite of its presumed fragility, is an organ of great stamina and resiliency, and what human being can resist doing something he knows he shouldn't?

Even the Cowardly Lion... roared once in a while!

Every so often, in his constant quest for improvement, the student will deliberately mistreat his voice.

Surprisingly enough, this can work to the student's advantage, and for any teacher to forbid this occasional emotional release for fear it might do harm to the instrument, is both useless and unnecessary.

"Sympathy Pains"

Attending vocal performances of any kind has always caused my larynx to react subliminally.

I have always felt these "Sympathy Pains," assimilating within my instrument, to be "user friendly"

Upon exiting the theatre after this experience and testing my own voice, I have found my own instrument to be much more flexible and "obedient"

Of course you realize this is only a temporary "fix"

Your instrument (obeying its own inclinations) will soon revert to its former obstinate state.

User-Friendly

All singers have a certain amount of trepidation concerning their "high notes." This is normal.

There is no reason to do what some of them do - become emotionally overwrought, imagining the worst scenario every time a "high note" looms above the staff.

The basic premise here remains... consider your voice, regardless of its imperfections, to be user-friendly.

Give a dog a good name - and it may forget how to bite!

Compliments

Even the most proficient of singers do not often compliment each other. It's nice to be praised, but they do not really need the approval of their peers. The audience will let them know, in no uncertain terms, how they fared. They are pros... they know their craft.

Now pause for a moment, and reflect upon those singers who, for obvious reasons, are not as praiseworthy. Whether 'tis an imagined rivalry, or a deep-seated need to feel superior (a combination of arrogance, jealousy, and insecurity) Hell will freeze over... before they verbally approve of anyone else's efforts.

Perhaps some deep rooted need for self-preservation overrides their charitable nature, and forbids them. I don't know.

All I know is that a little charity never hurt anyone.

Stammering

I only knew of one student in my formative years with this hesitant and repetitious speech pattern who has ever taken vocal lessons.

My teacher instinctively understood that it well may be a neurological phenomenon of some sort wherein a minor short - circuit contradicts the tongue's ability to perform.

She was adamantly insistent that anyone afflicted with this impediment must of necessity rid themselves of their penitent demeanor towards others and take charge.

Under her tutorial guidance he improved dramatically.

Otherwise, all I know about this minor impediment of the speech organs is that if a word begins with a vowel, it is far easier for a stutterer to pronounce it.

It well may be there are voice teachers who may benefit stammerers by teaching them systematic placement of consonants and a different way of thinking about articulation... I would hope so.

However, I'll put my money on a good speech therapist.

The Power of Imagination

Everyone has experienced the "battle royal" involved in trying to swallow an aspirin, or any other pill of similar ilk.

With a glass of water, it's bad enough, but… without?

Now the storm clouds gather.

I have always considered anything my taste buds disagreed with (in this context) to be… a jelly bean! When I was "short", I had no choice in the matter.

However, time marches on, and to this day, when swallowing a bitter pill, I still conjure up this sugar-coated taste of happiness.

(I much prefer licorice)

Nobody's Perfect

Singers forget, screw up, and ofttimes just do something stupid.

No singer is by any means perfect and being (contrary to public opinion) somewhat human, all singers make mistakes.

In practice, you must at all times attempt to correct anything gone awry.

In performance, you learn to give the impression that whatever occurs.. was meant to be. Chastise yourself later. Full speed ahead, and damn the torpedoes!

Any conscientious student will become flustered and ill at ease knowing he has "goofed"

There is no sense in allowing the audience to know this. The audience only realizes something is wrong when you let them know it!

Even if your mistake has been all too obvious, they will condone it if you do not make them feel ill at ease!

The last thing I want is "sympathetic" applause.

You must learn to make mistakes with authority.

Verbal Contracts

The knights of yesteryear were known as the Pure of Heart.

They were praised in poetry and song. Nothing could daunt them.

Their honor demanded absolute fidelity to their quest.

No power on earth could sway them from their sense of purpose.

Times change. Today, coupled with a good lawyer, one can "weasel" out of most anything.

You give your word... You Keep It!

Bundle it Up

In any performance, fate may conspire, and providence may not provide.

Witness the noted tenor, whose choice of roles sometimes forced him to wear a paste-on mustache (he couldn't grow a good one).

He gave up this particular bit of characterization after inhaling it... during his big aria!

Anything not nailed down during a performance will either fall apart, or get lost, strayed, or stolen.

(Of course this does not include the special problem of animals onstage... who may be inspired to leave a memento.)

Better Luck Next Time

No, 'tis not a locust invasion... just another hoard of sopranos descending en masse for that one part to be filled in the opera house.

Auditions like these are excruciating for all concerned.

All you can do is hope for the best.

There are just too many kittens for the titty!

P.S. At least one of the sopranos will cough up a fur ball!

Supertitles

There comes a time, when all good things come to an end. With all due modesty, I, who had always considered myself to be the one all-knowledgeable source, the final arbitrator for any, and every, pro or con situation… have thrown in the towel!

At the recent premiere of a new opera, I was forced to admit… that without the aid of the words above the proscenium, I would have been at a total loss as to what was transpiring on stage.

As fluent as I may have been in the language of this new opera, the singers were not! After all, who could blame them… they were singing in English!

Now, I understand the need for supertitles!

"With a Little Bit o' Luck"

A small black kitten had wandered into my backyard.

This miserable specimen of feline misfortune had been neglected, abandoned, and was obviously on her last legs.

A large abscess that ravaged her right eye precluded her ability to survive.

The veterinarian, a man of compassion, felt that putting her to "sleep" would be the merciful thing to do.

Well, I felt that the kitten would not readily agree with that decision, (after all, no one asked her opinion) so the vet operated on the eye; gave her all kinds of tender loving care for a few days, and lo and behold, one of the nurses became so enamored of this "poor wandering one", that she persuaded me to part with her, promising to provide a good home!

(I didn't offer any objections)

The kitten "lucked out" All she needed was a fighting chance.

"She opens her mout' too wide - See Dat?
Mout' like a cave - but what a voice!
What a voice - don't know how she does it
wit her mout' open like dat'n goin' all
over d'place - Mudder Natur' Dats how…

Maybe ten years, she won't have a voice left-
but what-a singiozzo!"

NARRATIVO

The Narrativo that I have included in this volume is a condensed version of well over 200 lessons I had managed to save on tape for reference and nostalgic reasons. I have "reanimated" most of the principles I adhere to in order to acquaint the student with some semblance of what he should expect during the course of a lesson.

Of course, I was forced to condense and clean up most of this material into a more realistic format, and moreover, restrain myself from belaboring the point any more than absolutely necessary.

Yes, it really happened… I've got the tapes to prove it!

What is the "operatic voice"? When people talk about an operatic voice they are talking about a voice that has at least two of three characteristics: placement, amplitude, and ease of tessitura.

Having one or more of these as gifts from Mother Nature - an inborn amplitude, an instinctive placement, a naturally easy "top"- may make the untrained or partly trained student sound prematurely "operatic" and may thereby garner him or her certain extra advantages: early performance experience, through early opportunities such as choir solos and parts in local productions; the ability to win vocal competitions at an early age; and, above all, the confidence that comes from early and continuing encouragement from peers, parents, teachers, choir directors, etc.

These advantages can contribute to a successful career - yes.

They can also be a terrible pitfall for the student who comes to believe that those early-rewarded gifts from Mother Nature are adequate substitutes for correct technique and thorough training.

They are not! By themselves, they aren't likely to take you to the very top (where all singers, no matter what they say, long to be) and, if they do, they won't keep you there long.

Your voice, beautiful and half-trained, won't be able to stand it. A rapid rise and fall is the best you can hope for. More likely, without serious effort to improve what you have been given, you the "gifted" student will spend your life as a big duck in a little pond, star of the local production and soloist in the local church choir, applauded at 40 by the same folks who applauded when you were 14.

Or, you can admit here and now that to be born talented is not to be born perfect. And you can work. And go to the very top and stay there.

Now, what about the "nongifted" student? What hope is there for the student whose natural range seems limited, whose amplitude appears deficient, whose placement is "out of whack", who, in short has nothing but a burning desire to sing to recommend him?

About as much hope as there is for a "gifted" student, as long as he's willing to work his ass off. Short of actual congenital defects, there is no vocal problem that can't be "solved" with a good technique.

136

Range is developed through proper articulation: using consonants and vowels correctly to"place" the voice without strain on any given pitch. The development of range - especially in the upper part of a students' tessitura - in turn develops the resonance, or amplitude, of the voice.

And as the voice grows in range and amplitude, continued correct placement of vowels and consonants ensures that the full voice is projected out and to the back row of the house. That's opera, doc.

To recapitulate:

1- Consonants and vowels are the key to developing placement.

2- Placement is the key to developing the range.

3- Developing the range is the key to developing the resonance.

4- The operatic voice is just a voice with fully developed resonance.

5- Operatic technique is the awareness of how resonance is developed.

The following "Narrativo" is the story of two students, each an unsuccessful nongradute of two or more previous teachers, each with a voice that could charitably have been described as problematical. Both had a burning desire to sing. Neither had been stars of the high-school musical or soloists in the high school chorus. Hell, the soprano couldn't even get into the high-school choir. They were perfect subjects for a course in how to develop a technique, and a voice, almost from scratch.

The soprano had been taught as a mezzo by two different teachers neither of whom had ever taken her above an A flat in an aria or song, and the second of whom never took her that "high" even in an exercise. She had struggled through the "lowest" of the songs in the Italian Song Book, Cherubino's, Siebel's and an assortment of downward-transposed German, French, and English art-songs.

And, now for the coup-de grace… what you have been reading are the private thoughts of the soprano in question.

When I first came to Pete, this so-called mezzo-contralto's "low" notes were inaudible, my "middle voice"- supposedly my glory - was weak, ragged, out of tune and colorless.

Pete took me up to D above high C in my first exercise, gave me "Caro nome "as my first aria, and our Narrativo proceeds from there..

My teacher loved the old Italian classic songs. When done right, they are beautiful. I went through "Caro Mio Ben"," Pieta,Signore "and" Vittoria, Vittoria"… that's all. All the rest were hung out to dry.

As student material, these three songs were made to serve one particular purpose. They were only used to teach me how to enunciate, articulate, and pronounce in Italian.

They were absolutely useless for extending the range of my voice or giving me any semblance of comfort with what I was doing. She and I knew damned well I couldn't do justice to any of them.

Why do teachers keep their students on this kind of material for years?

Very simple! They're not teaching their students how to sing… only how to interpret!

The basses will never sing anything above an E, the baritones to maybe an F sharp, the tenors to maybe an A flat, and the poor sopranos will never go above an A natural!

And yet they absolutely believe they're learning how to sing.

And that's not the worst of it…

The worst is that half the teachers around can't tell what the hell kind of a potential a student has to begin with!

This basso was referred to me. He was getting desperate - over a period of five years, he had studied with five teachers. All had spoon fed him the standard diet and a couple of them were venturesome enough to include an aria or two. They also concurred, that he had without a doubt, an uncommonly good bass voice. However, after all this time, he still couldn't manage to achieve and to hold on to a decent F natural. That meant that half the bass repertoire, stuff like Don Giovanni, was denied him.

Fifteen minutes into the first lesson I told him… "I don't give a damn how the hell good you or your teachers think the lower part of your tessitura is… I'm a tenor… and I can sing low F's better than you can! You're no bass… you're a baritone!"

I brought him up to A flats, and at the end of the lesson he was walking on air. All he needed was a little light… at the end of the tunnel.

You tell me… how in hell can all five of these miscreants honestly continue to "teach" voice!

Tay Awe Tay Awe Tay going up the 12 note scale on a triad is the first exercise I ever sang. The first consonant I ever sang was a T.

Since the T is pinpointed against the ridge above your front teeth, which is the center of the focus of resonance in all voices, this helps you to get some sensation or feeling of placement.

I got a little dizzy the first time I ever sang a C, so if it rattles your brains a little... that's good.

Your voice thins out and goes a little haywire above a G natural, but you're not a mezzo... you're a soprano. Even though the upper part of your tessitura hasn't got any redeeming qualities.. there's an illusion of a much darker essence or timbre in your voice than is customary with sopranos.

I think you've got a big spinto buried in there somewhere.

Sopra.

You don't want me to sing? You just want me to say it?

That's all I ever want you to do for anything!

Sopra.

You mean literally and figuratively?

Every which way you can... to parlate, to recite, to narrate, to talk to me. I must be able to understand the message you are trying to deliver. The words are as important as the melodic line. I don't ever want you to sacrifice the consonant or distort the vowel because of the pitch.

We know where Larry and Curly are... but we can't find Moe! He's wandered off some place. Let's see if we can't coax him back. I'll tempt him musically with my three-fingered triads. You keep calling out his name, he's bound to hear you sooner or later.

We'll start on F natural.

As good as your OH vowel may have been in this scale, I want a better one. I want an OH vowel with all the focus and concentration you can bring to bear on it. I want an OH that rhymes with MOE that rhymes with TOE that is out there six yards in front of your nose! I want a definitive OH... no half-breed OH's, no undernourished OH's.

I want an OH vowel with claws!

Caro Nome to be spoken... not sung... on complete arpeggios, in every variation you can possibly improvise.

Ca - a   ro   No - o - o - me   Ca - ro   No - me - e - e - e

Now we're going to dwell a moment on the "C". It's a harsh breath sound against the front wall of the mouth. The tongue comes into play, but I don't want you to ever think of the tongue assisting this consonant in any way. Your tongue will find its own way to assist the air flow that you must mentally direct somewhere around the vicinity of the ridge above your front teeth.

Now don't misunderstand me.. when I say a harsh breath sound, it does not mean you have to karate-chop it. If I hear a harsh breath, that means you are using too much air. Any vowel preceded by a C, K, or a Q, must of necessity be there mentally, before you bring forth any of these three consonants. Now the AWE vowel preceded by a harsh breath sound may well be the dominant call of the crow. Who's to say it isn't? So you're now a big sassy crow. When I snap my fingers, you immediately respond with a Caw. Just talk to me... don't sing anything. The pitch doesn't matter! When I say talk to me... I mean just that.

Once you begin to believe you're singing instead of speaking, you feel you have to "do" something. No you do not!

Why create any more problems than you already have?

Sopra.

Can I sing down low that way?

There's no such thing as low and high, it's all in the same place. I know that's hard to believe, but on any pitch, any note you sing, the center of vibrations is all on the upper lip as far as your vowel is concerned.

Did you know all the vowels are on your lips? No?

Sopra.

I was taught that the vowels were on the tongue, in the mouth.

Mother's Milk! No wonder your words are schmeary.

Mouth-singing inhibits the flexibility of your tongue by making you tone-conscious instead of word-conscious, so your voice will never sound really forward.

O.K. We'll go back to the Caro Nome arpeggio and all I want you to do now is to kiss each vowel goodbye. Wave them on their way.

======

Sopra.

I was taught to show my teeth, my first teacher said it helped to get up high.

Acc.

Yeah, a lot of coloraturas say that... you're taught to smile.

Yes, it works, but for the wrong reasons. It makes you think you're inducing a form of vibratory response within your sinus and nasal passages. It's purely psychological.

You get the same result - that is, augmenting your nasal resonance - by sniffing or smelling a flower.

The tyranny behind this misconception is the idea that you will always have to take special measures to insure the delivery of your "high notes ". That's where strain and stress come from.

I always cringe a little when a soprano deliberately assumes a toothy expression in the upper part of her tessitura.

I get the impression of a predator on the prowl... seeking the nearest available throat to sink her fangs into!

141

Sopra.

What?

I said stay there!

Sopra.

You mean to keep doing whatever it is I'm doing?

Yes. You haven't had enough experience to recognize when your voice is doing the best it can or when it's working with you.

Now when you see yourself in the mirror you can tell immediately when you are opening your mouth too much. You ran that last scale without moving anything except the tip of your tongue.

You did everything the way you're supposed to.

I know it took damn near the whole lesson but all I've been trying to do is give you a sense of purpose in what you're doing and to try to counteract some of the gooney-bird principles you've been saddled with by your former teachers.

So, whenever I tell you to stay there… you know you're right!

=========

Sopra.

Was that an E flat that I held?

No, no… you're not holding a note! What are you holding?

Sopra.

A vowel!

And what is that vowel?

Sopra.

Ah.

A-W-E! What is d'awe?

Sopra.

D'amor!

What the hell does D'amor mean? If you skim over the consonant all you have left is the vowel. If the vowel doesn't mean anything to you, it becomes a mere tone. When you start thinking "tone" you get nervous about your pitch. It's a vicious circle. Just give me the word D'amor.

You're still thinking the pitch is higher than it really is.

Don't open your mouth any more than you have to, Mother Nature will do it for you. Every time you try to accommodate the pitch in this manner, you automatically shift gears, and lose your placement.

I don't know what it is with those singers that feel compelled to open their mouths like a drawbridge. Most of them, after a few years, lose what they had to begin with, and their voices either become hollow and lackluster or they seem to bottle everything up inside themselves even as they strive to look as if they were letting it all hang out!

Hell, I won't deny there are those voices that can flout all the rules... and still survive. How they get away with it... I don't know.

Whether I go to heaven or hell... that well may be the day I find out!

Anyway, since most voices are not born to survive a botched technique imitating those few that get away with it is never a good idea.

———

You're going down with the pitch, thinking it's lower than it really is.

Just as it's wrong to think high and go up with the pitch, it's just as destructive of the voice to go "down" and think "low".

I don't want you to DO anything at all as far as the lower part of your tessitura is concerned. You spent three years with this other teacher working on your "lower register"... and it only got worse.

So... what is, or isn't there, doesn't matter. Any conscious or deliberate attempt to make or create a bigger or stronger sound below your middle C only reinforces all the problems you had to begin with.

Leave it alone!

———

Hold on a moment. You're doing it again. Every time you poke your nose into the score, you end up singing to the printed page.

If you have to look at the score, sing through it! Otherwise you lose your forward momentum. Instead of letting your voice and your imagination deliver the message, you subconsciously tie it down or chain it to the music stand.

That's the prime reason why church choirs sound so sterile. No one sings beyond the end of their nose!

Naturally the middle part of your voice is much warmer than the rest of it, that's to be expected… after all, that's the only part of your voice you've ever used.

Since you've never worked the upper part of your tessitura before, these strange new sensations you are beginning to feel, are the direct result of new sympathetic vibrations coming into play.

Since everything on earth vibrates in some way or other… your heads no different than anything else. The more these vibrations expand and multiply, the more resonant your voice becomes.

The only thing we can do is to make these new vibrations as welcome as possible…give them all the squatter's rights they feel they need. Your voice may sound screechy and harsh to you, but that`s because all these new vibrations are squabbling like tomcats over territorial rights. Sooner or later… they'll get together, and start harmonizing with each other. That's the way Mother Nature works.

As far as the present quality of your voice is concerned, pay no attention to it. You've got more important things to worry about!

———

Sopra.

It doesn't feel right… it sounds awful…

Well, you managed to get the D… it's starting to come in.

I just don't understand why your former teacher never corrected you about opening your mouth too much.

Sopra.

I never went above an A with her, except maybe once or twice.

Oh boy… you can't open your mouth that much… you've no place to go… the more you open your mouth, the more you waste! You not only sacrifice your vowel, you also lose what placement you have.

The more you open your mouth, the more you go out of place. Only open your mouth when you feel you absolutely have to.

You'll get used to it. You don't want you to look like a fish out of water… do you?

Voice teachers have a tendency to place more obstacles in your path than they get rid of. As good as some of them may be, most are saddled by concepts that do more to destroy than to give birth.

Since no singer, dead or alive, has ever known what the hell was going on in his or her larynx, voice box, instrument... call it what you want... while singing, they have all conjured up images, both mental and physical, to describe what they thought they were doing.

Since they've never seen the process in action, their margin of error is more or less 100 %.

Too many voice teachers encourage students to dwell on their bodily functions as singers even when those functions are involuntary.

This creates self-consciousness where none should be necessary, and that in turn creates tension, which is the last thing you need.

So, while we're taking a break here, I want you to understand why a sense of focus OUTSIDE rather than inside your voice is a prime directive. A picture may be worth a thousand words, but a picture of a larynx isn't worth the paper it's printed on.

While it may be true in a scientific sense that the center of resonance in every voice is just above the larynx, thinking about it in this manner will only defeat our purpose, which is to get your voice out of your throat and into the theater - preferably to the back row of seats, not the front one.

Therefore we must try to direct or pinpoint the sound someplace as far out and away from us as possible... where it feels comfortable.

The instrument will always relax, even under external pressure, when an image of internal freedom is achieved. A little relaxation goes a long way.

Now, since the lips are the end of the vocal apparatus or tube, we try to imagine that the vowel is at the end of the lips!

What could be simpler? It works. Why complicate things?

When you are singing somewhat correctly, your upper lip tends to vibrate once in a while, because, as my teacher explained it to me, the upper lip carries the weight of the vowel.

Of course, in order to keep the vowel alive and able to renew itself, you have to have breath pressure behind it, that's fundamental. But you don't fuss about the breath, you don't worry about the breath, whatever you use up is constantly being replenished by Mother Nature, so you forget about it.

Your vocal cords are not working in a vacuum. They operate involuntarily. They're always "on stand-by", and will automatically tense for any pitch you may conceive... whether you sing it or not.

When you wake up in the morning, it's only natural that you are going to stumble around for a few minutes. It's the same with your voice. Whenever you warm up and try to tune your instrument, you are really testing the perimeters of what your voice is capable of, at that moment.

Whether your voice goes or not, doesn't matter. Whether you sound good, bad, or indifferent, doesn't matter. It's not a matter of life or death! All you want to do is to get some of the kinks out.

Don't fuss over it, I'm not expecting you to light up the studio.

———————

When you know exactly how and what you are going to do, your instrument will obey you, like a good puppy dog... otherwise, it gets confused.

More specifically, unless you know exactly what you are going to do with your consonant and your vowel, they will exert a negative "pull" on your instrument. When this happens, your instrument gets confused as to your true intentions... and tries to compensate with unnecessary extra physical effort for your lapse in mental effort.

Well, I don't have to tell you what happens next, do I?

Give me a vowel and a consonant, don't worry about the tessitura. You don't ever concern yourself about the pitch involved because it's subconscious... you get the words, you get the pitch automatically... unless of course... you didn't completely memorize it... right?

———————

No. You are not flat on "Quando", just a little under the pitch. The same thing happens to "Core". Basically, not only is your vowel at fault, but also your harsh breath C and Q consonants.

If your AWE vowel or your OH vowel is not there mentally prior to sounding the C or the Q consonant, and your C and Q consonants are slow or slovenly, together, they seem to somehow drag the pitch down.

Each helps the other to sound duller or unrehearsed.

All right… I'm going to become a little pedantic. If I sound a little preachy… just grin and bear it.

A voice is a mechanism. Even though your personality may enter into it, your voice, your instrument must be trained as a SEPARATE entity. It has laws governing its progress and these laws are always being bollixed up and subverted by the singer's emotional upheavals.

Although your voice may exist in a symbiotic relationship with your ego, it is imperative that, in training (acquiring a technique) you be able to disassociate your voice, your larynx, your instrument, from the persona you believe yourself to be.

The required technical knowledge must be acquired before an artistic approach can be unleashed.

Only a logical and common sense approach can improve whatever you have to work with physically.

And, naturally, the kindred spirit or desire within you to excel in what you are being taught will, in time, modify and enhance your own artistic nature…

I should hope so…

———————————

Ah, what have we here… a hand motion that goes around in circles? Are you aboard ship waving goodbye to those on shore?

When you make a motion of any kind, it must be a definitive motion, no wishy-washy motions! Otherwise, it looks like you are trying to thumb a ride, signal the waiter… or trying to catch flies.

Sopra.

It's draining my energy trying to think of stuff to do with my hands…

Ah yes… you are relying more on your gut instinct to survive than any hand or body motions you may have practiced, and believe me, every motion you make while singing takes a helluva lot of practice to perfect.

First you have to determine what two or three hand and body motions seem to be the most natural for you… then impose the same discipline upon them as you did on your voice… in the meantime, make a hand motion only when you feel compelled to… and then make it as slow as you possibly can.

Why did you stop?

Sopra.

That was awful!

Ah ha! There you go again, judging yourself as you go along, imagining the worst! Alright, right now your voice does sound a little hard- edged or strident... so what! Just because your instrument isn't up to par, you can't allow your emotions to intensify whatever wrongs you think you may have committed.

Sopra.

Well, if you think this sounds bad now, you should have heard it earlier this week... there wasn't anything there.

You're working at this moment with an impaired instrument.

Sopra.

What's the matter with it?

It's in a period of transition. It's trying to establish a new dominance within itself. It's like a snake shedding its skin... it's growing bigger and stronger.

No matter what it feels like, or sounds like, that's what you're working with.

The good part about it, is that you're getting better! If you were not... this would never happen.

───────────────

Everything you've been doing so far sounds pretty good, so I really shouldn't fuss, but you should know by now I want the maximum your instrument is capable of. Let's go back to basics. I want you to put your paw out there and tell me what you are holding.

Sopra.

My larynx!

Right! However, if you wish to imagine a tweety bird in your hand, that can be just as proficient in bringing your voice out to where it belongs...

all well and good. Whatever seems to work for you.

Yes, your instrument is in a state of imbalance. It has, as far as I know, an increased tension in one part of it and a decreased tension in another.

Your larynx is actually opening up some more.

It has to! It doesn't know any other way to go.

Mother Nature is coming to your rescue.

However, Mother Nature is also doing you a disservice. She is penalizing you. You want something? It will cost you! Nothings free. Your voice is going to feel a bit strange to you, not at all like what you are accustomed to, and you are also going to sound like hell for a few days.

That's a cheap enough price to pay!

Sopra.

...The whole thing feels lower!

Well, that's what we're working for. You're not reaching for the B and the C like you used to. Any time you think that way, you're chasing a "will o`the wisp". You're reaching up there to pull the clouds down... but there's nothing up there to grab hold of.

You're better off chasing rainbows, they're a lot more tangible.

Who knows? Maybe there is a pot of gold at the end of one.

Sopra.

Now I'm all confused... I don't know where I am...

This aria is goofy... it wanders all over the place and even I don't know where the hell you are.

Acc.

Well... I must admit... even I made a few mistakes. What say we take a break here... and share the blame equally?

You're still too apprehensive on your A flats. They may be a bit hard-

edged and they lack the necessary warmth, but they're a lot more substantial than they used to be. Basically, you're still cringing or drawing back, folding into yourself.

Here, take this deck of cards. I want to see you deal them out like this...

Here's one for you sir... it's the consonant T, here's one for you sir...

a beautiful OH vowel, here's one for you sir..a resplendent F sharp. With six players in this game you're going to have to deal out 30 cards. Since you have the order of the cards memorized, all you have to do is to deal them out.

If you're going to give them away... give them away!

The audience doesn't have to like the hand you're dealing them, but so what!... they're stuck with it.

Just stand tall and augment everything!

I don't really know why some singers do not consciously wish to be understood. Would it perhaps make them more vulnerable to an audience? Now this soprano we just heard singing Donna Anna is a perfect example of what I'm talking about.

I couldn't understand any of her words except in the recitatives. As soon as she was required to "sing", she became incomprehensible.

Hell, even I couldn't tell whether her consonants smeared up her vowels or whether her vowels smeared up her consonants.

What she did was suggest the words, nothing more, and the way she was moving her mouth around... I thought she was chewing tobacco!

All in all, I got bored trying to figure out what she was grumbling about.

Sopra.

May be she was taught that good diction, at some point, HAS to be sacrificed in order to maintain a beautiful tone.

Could very well be. But you'll never have that problem. You know damn well good diction, at ALL points, has to be practiced in order to achieve one.

You were listening to yourself.

Sopra.

Is that what I was doing?

150

Yes, you were listening so hard to yourself, you allowed your instrument to take over. That's the same as looking over your shoulder while you're driving... sooner or later you're going to run off the road and crack up!

And you sure as hell wouldn't try flying an airplane that way either!

Listening to yourself while you are singing is a fault most teachers are not even aware of, or wouldn't call a fault even if they knew. Why shouldn't the student listen to himself... after all, how else can he possibly monitor or correct his mistakes, if he doesn't hear what he is doing?

The bottom line in any performance is that no matter what you may just have done or tried to do with the music... it's over with!

I've seen a helluva lot of performers with their heads tilted sideways... it's a bad habit, and they can't get out of it; they are more interested in what they have just done, or are just doing than what they are going to do next!

When you listen to yourself, you lose your spontaneity, you lose half of what you've got to work with.

At this stage of the game, your ear, and the sensations you feel, are going to fool you anyway.

So I can't impress this upon you enough. You don't ever give a God Damn... how or what you THINK you sound like... Period!

Running "Caro Nome "up and down the scales has given you a feeling of familiarity with these two words, but you're making three words out of two. Caro is fine, but you're singing nome as two words... nome-may. You're dwelling too long on the M, and you are taking for granted your AY vowel will be there. My only concern at this moment is for the authenticity of your Italian.

So, no singing allowed... that's what gets you into trouble!

Just talk to me... the pitch is subconscious!

You have to learn how to cope with what you've got. You have no choice in the matter… you're not a recording. The elements of chance guarantee only one thing… that there are no guarantees!

There's no way in hell you can become an irresistible force unless you are willing to take whatever risks are necessary.

If everything you sing could be preordained to your satisfaction with nothing left to chance, nothing ventured beyond your present skills, where's the gamble..how the hell are you going to get better?

Yes, I understand your voice is now going through a change, a flux of some sort within itself and you feel that every once in a while it's going to take a bite out of you… par for the course.

You're now learning how to recognize these warning signs and learning how to take the proper precautions.

Since your body is your instrument, you have no choice… all you can do is sweat it out… don't quibble about it..don't fuss about it!

Keep your eye on the sparrow… just do the best you can.

No, you're thinking the pitch as being higher than it really is again. Remember what I told you in the last lesson about all these singers who were taught to sing vertically… they go up and down with the pitch like an escalator.

There's no such thing as high and low. Everything's straight out.

Think horizontal! Straight out! That way your tongue won't have this tendency to go up with the pitch any more than it has to.

Remember… nothing above… and nothing below… your shoulders.

Just because you're a big spinto, doesn't mean you cannot sing the coloratura repertoire. Coloratura sopranos bore me to death! It's a very rare occasion that I hear a voice in this category that actually wants to communicate, or is trained to deliver the text.

Their prime directive seems to consist of running scales and chirping away pleasantly. Who could ask for anything more?

Sopra.

That's all I can do.

Acc.

That wasn't bad, but you certainly could have gone much higher.

Sopra.

Could I have?

Acc.

Yes, but you started thinking how high the pitch was and you started flinching at it. When you had that practice session with the flutist you didn't have any problems getting an F above C.

Maybe you are too self-conscious about what you have or haven't got as far as this aria is concerned. I think you may be reverting subconsciously back to the time when you were first trying to learn this aria.

What you have learned in the past year or so has now become so ingrained in your subconscious, that your voice is doing what it has to do… but in a minor way you have carried over some of the bugaboo problems we originally had with this song, and so you're reverting.

Don't worry about it, we'll just iron it all out again.

———————————

You started out great, I didn't believe what I heard. As soon as you sang the B flat, you listened so damned hard to it, everything came to a screeching halt.

You can't criticize yourself this way. You criticize yourself this way in front of an audience, you'll never get through the aria.

Don't magnify all the little trivialities you think may be wrong with it out of proportion to their importance.

I won't deny that there may be someone in the audience that knows Vissi D'arte as well as you do. So what! Let them sing it!

Nobody's perfect!

Good… but no cigar! You give me the impression that Rusalka is talking to her pillow…

When you say "Tell me, o pale, pale moon "you are not talking to yourself… you are talking to the moon! Where the hell is the moon? It's out there… way out there.

I don't know whether the moon would be interested in what you have to say or not, but you sure as hell have to get its attention!

You have to be more adamant!

Don't plead with it… demand an answer!

O.K. I've mentioned this before and I'll mention it again. Your voice is the same as this cigarette lighter I'm holding in my hand.

You flip the switch and it lights. Of course it sometimes takes a couple of flips to get it going… just like an outboard motor.

So, since your physical voice is not a part of your personality, you must treat it as a separate entity. There's no point in inflicting undue stress and strain upon your instrument by subjugating it to your personal and private phobias.

Its job is hard enough as it is without the two of you engaging in a tug of war.

Too damn much practice time is lost - and, later, too many opportunities are lost - by singers who flip their voices once, and, if they don't start up right away, decide the skirmish is not worth it and resolve not to go boating at all. Don't be afraid to sound bad… or you'll never sound as good as you could.

I know it's a strange feeling to be holding a conversation with yourself on stage, but you're going to have to be a helluva lot more emphatic in what you're trying to say to convince me you're not just muttering in your beer.

No matter how private your character's thoughts may be, every recitativo needs an outside force to communicate with.. so talk to me.

One thing more. No eavesdropping. Don't listen to yourself!

Well, you certainly didn't finish this aria in a blaze of glory.

You ran that last scale like you were running for your life. That AWE vowel of yours not only lost its identity… it was seeking asylum!

Slow down a bit. You're in a hurry to make a mistake. Just because you lose your self-confidence is no reason to speed things up. Getting through this song sooner won't make it better.

You lost your authority… you knew it, and you showed it.

Let's take the whole thing from the beginning again. Your voice is all right..

Don't worry about your musicianship. You're taking it so fast you haven't got time… but your voice is holding up.

Acc:

I've heard a thousand amateur pianists who always take the scales faster than they can do them. I don`t know what damned reason they have for doing it, but they take them faster than the rest of the piece. There is nothing wrong with slowing up a scale… it gives you more time to think about it.

Yes, that's true. Your voice doesn't sound smeared at all; each consonant and vowel are where they belong… but musically… it's another story. You are not doing justice to the aria.

Acc.

Yes, speeding up makes it seem like the notes are wrong, but they are actually not wrong… try a little meditation on your scales.

Okay, you're running into trouble again. Your anxieties are beginning to overwhelm your instrument. We'll just back off a bit and give them something a little more tangible to grumble about. I want you to grab hold of the back of a chair. Now I want you to pick it straight up… hold it straight out… and feel the weight of it. Alright… now I want you to put it down slowly.

Do you remember how it feels… The weight of it?

This time, I want you to hold that chair out in front of you feeling the weight of it… without actually holding the chair!

You're not always going to have something concrete to clutch while you sing, so this is just an exercise that will temporarily alleviate your angst.

It's all right. I know your cold interferes and you're snuffling up a storm, but since we're subjecting your instrument to stress under these conditions and it's still fluctuating from that vocal change you had last week, it will probably take another few days for it to return to normal and relish its new found freedom.

I know what you are going through. The muscle memory response is a very powerful force. It almost feels like the Russian army taking up residence in your throat.

It's nothing more than a desperate rear guard action by the muscles in your larynx refusing to give way to new concepts or ideas.

I remember the time when another soprano's instrument bobbled on an A natural and I just happened to catch it. You might say her instrument had just readjusted its internal muscular structure to coordinate a better balance within itself.

I've had these vocal changes occur time and time again. Now you're beginning to understand how to handle it. Sooner or later the new voice irons itself out. It's Mother Nature's way.

Oscar, being a typical teen-ager, revels in being the center of attention. Nothing else in life gives him as much pleasure. Now Oscar knows something no one else does… "If you guess the secret word… you win a hundred dollars! But, only I know the secret word."

That's what "Saper Vorreste "is all about… that's what you have to put across. You're teasing every one!

E natural above C… and sounding almost half-way decent… for a big voice like yours, that's damned good!

Sopra.

I've got a trick now… the "higher" you make me go, the further away I have to sing it! First I sing to your cat on the fence, then I sing to that sailboat out on the water, then I sing to the top of that mountain!

That's great! The more you think of going out, the easier it all gets. You're breaking down the old habits of thinking up or going high for the pitch.

Sopra.

My accompanist feels that some of these coloratura songs and arias are wrong for me... on the tape my voice sounds much too heavy for them.

That's why I gave them to you. Another teacher would have had you singing a much heavier repertoire, before you were ready for it.

There's nothing wrong with a big voice like yours singing the pure lyric Bellini and Donizetti stuff. A bigger voice always gives a more dramatic thrust to the lyric repertoire than the usual bunch of sopranos that sing it.

More often than not, you are going to hear sopranos doing much heavier stuff than their voices are capable of.

Just because you're a big spinto, doesn't mean you cannot sing the coloratura repertoire. Coloratura sopranos bore me to death!

It's a very rare occasion that I hear a voice in this category that actually wants to communicate, or is trained to deliver the text.

Their prime directive seems to consist of running scales and chirping away pleasantly. Who could ask for anything more?

As long as you feel you can do justice to the repertoire you are doing...

the sky's the limit!

Your instrument has finally warmed up... it's no longer sleeping on the job... that was a good "Saper Vorreste".

Sopra.

Yes, it feels like I've got a whole lot of room in there, but it also feels like it's kind of ricocheting around in there and doesn't want to settle down.

I think that's because your focus of resonance is trying to realign or reestablish itself. Your instrument, the larynx and the muscles inside your voice box, are past the point of no return... they've been balky and a bit obstinate this past hour but now they have compromised a bit and are willing to go along with what you want.

Or... perhaps Mother Nature has infected you with a little bit of "Joie de Vivre", some enthusiasm for what you're doing. That also accounts for a helluva whole lot!

Sopra.

My voice doesn't feel right... it feels bad... it's barely there.

Well, you haven't sung, practiced, or studied anything for a couple of weeks, so your instrument's still asleep. We'll just keep prodding it... it'll wake up. You can't really blame it for not cooperating... it's been on vacation too!

I should hope you've learned by now that just because your voice may feel good, does not mean you are going to sing well. That's a crock! And, needless to say, when your voice is giving the best it can... you really don't feel anything at all.

One more thing before we begin again; this piece of music we've been plowing through has its own set of rules. It's new and unfamiliar territory to you. All we can do is harness what you've got to work with and hope for the best.

Hold on a minute... just because you're running a good scale, your voice wants to go, and you're happy with the results... that's not good enough!

"Separa" is one word. I don't hear "separa", I hear three different syllables. Don't divide the word up. I want your scale to make sense. I don't care what kind of a scale you want to negotiate, what kind of word or phrase you want to get the kinks out of... it must mean something to you! What the hell's the point, if no one else can understand what you're trying to communicate?

These other bastards will have you run vowels all day long. Big deal!

Vowels, by themselves... don't accomplish anything.

You're not forceful enough. "Caro Nome" may begin as a meditation, but you can't meditate too! Mezza voce demands a softer thought, but you cannot in any way diminish the intensity required.

In a small hall you can get away with it, but, in the opera house, you'll never cut through the orchestra.

I want you to imagine... Gualtier Malde... you horny bastard...

you dirty rat...

My, oh my, oh my... you've managed to touch an F above C... not bad at all! Of course it isn't very good... but that don't make no never mind, it's beginning to come in.

What you have at this moment is a two-stage voice... in other words, you shift gears mentally. You are opening your mouth too much on the B flat and the C and that gives you nowhere to go. Because you feel you need more room for the higher tessitura involved, you feel the need for more space in your instrument. That doesn't work!

Another teacher would say that you are carrying your chest voice or your middle register up into your head voice. That's garbage!

The more you open your mouth... the sooner your vowel will disintegrate. Now your instrument compensates for this as long as it can, but it finally has to realign itself.

All we can do is to work on the upper part of your tessitura the way we've been doing... the stronger it gets, the easier everything else becomes.

I don't want you to think up! I want you to think OUT!

Sopra.

What? Wrong already!

You're singing like a little girl... I don't want you to be a little girl!

Sopra.

No... I'm a little boy!

Oh, that's why you're backing off. You never back off from anything... unless of course, it's a wild bull moose!

Sopra

Oh I see... my Cherubino was too namby pamby.

Yes. You can't ever come out weak and get stronger... it doesn't quite go.

It robs you of authority... your authority disappears.

Come out swinging... then if you wish to, you can back off.

Sopra.

I'm worried about my breath. I feel I'm going to do some damage to my small rib cage and everything like that, I just never seem to have enough breath to get through this aria.

That's only natural! You're still stumbling through it. You don't really know what to do with this aria… you don't know it that well. Once you have it down pat, and have no qualms about performing it, the breath is automatically given to you… you'll have all the breath you'll ever need for it. Trust me.

———

Sopra.

This time the B flat felt really good…

I'm glad to hear that… do you know why it felt so good?

Sopra.

Why?

Because your tongue didn't come up! By thinking horizontally instead of vertically, your tongue felt no inclination whatsoever to participate in what you were doing. This is precisely what all those other teachers would call having an "open throat"!

Now you are beginning to understand the tyranny behind the word "high" when used during the course of a lesson.

———

No matter how well you know the music, you can still get thrown for a loop.

I remember this baritone being chastised by the conductor after a concert performance. He questioned the baritone as to why he had missed his cue. The baritone explained that it really wasn't his fault at all… the bassoonist hadn't played his cue like he was supposed to. The conductor then informed the baritone that there was, indeed, a good reason for the bassoonist's oversight.

They didn't have a bassoonist in the orchestra!

Learn to count!

Well… your French is of the boulevards; I won't fuss about it… but when it comes to scales, I don't care if you are singing in Lower Slobovian, you must give me a definitive vowel, otherwise your vowel will assume any color it can reasonably hope to negotiate and eventually self-destruct.

Sopra.

I see. In order to keep my vowel as pure as possible I must continue to define it on every pitch of the scale…

Absolutely!

Sopra.

and if I keep modifying the vowel to make it "easier" for me as I go up or down it will eventually self-destruct and destroy my scale as well.

Absolutely! Part of achieving "an even scale "is being able to maintain a consistent vowel. So, whenever you run a scale, whatever vowel you pick… you stick to!

===

Sopra.

I can hear it banging… I can't stop it from banging!

The Q is a harsh breath sound against the front wall of the mouth… it has to bang just like your other harsh breath consonants. Sopra.

But you told me not to bang it…

Yes, that's true, but you are bracing for your entrance on the A flats and therefore your Quante has too much force behind it… you're punching it out.

I wasn't going to stop you, but if you don't like what it feels like or sounds like… good… we'll fix it right now!

===

I don't want to hear a beautiful Quando, a beautiful M'en, a beautiful Vo!

I don't want to hear beautiful tone. What I want to hear is Beautiful Truth!

Just tell it like it is. Talk to me!

Sopra.

Somehow or other the piano always seems to make my voice shriller… why is this?

It happens to everyone in the world. The piano is not really compatible with the human voice but since it's balanced in such a way so as to produce all the notes necessary, plus the accompaniment, it's the cheapest substitute for an orchestra you can buy.

Many years ago a violinist at the school needed someone to practice with.

I was bumbling my way through the tenor aria from Faust… so we agreed to bumble together.

I was amazed. Everything became easier. Somehow the violin made me soar and for the first time in my life I felt free… unchained…

Since you have no choice in the matter, try to ignore the piano as much as possible… don't listen too slavishly to it, use it only for your cues.

Sopra.

I found out that if I play everything an octave lower than what I am singing… I don't feel so intimidated.

Right… smart girl!

[Pete: The reason being the timbre of the piano, which is sharp and loud, without a lot of sympathetic vibrations. Pianos have no spin on them. Even thick chords with plenty of pedal on them don't turn over like the single notes of a wind or bowed string instrument.

You might point this out… your penitent proofer J. A.]

(You just did)

When you subconsciously "brace" for a pitch, your instrument can't help but flinch and close up slightly. I know you can't help it, but since your voice is doing the best it can with the tessitura you are demanding of it, I won't quibble.

Most singers do not understand, that trouble with a "high note "starts not with that note but with the notes below it.

Each word and each individual phrase has to be methodically "ironed out "in the lower part of the tessitura leading up to the pitch in question. Otherwise, the little jigsaw pieces of the puzzle not bonded together correctly become stumbling blocks... and you sure as hell are going to trip yourself up.

I know you're not too comfortable in this part of your tessitura.

We could for learning purposes take all your arias down a note or two and fake it, but that would defeat our ultimate purpose.

What we're going for is the sense of placement you must have to survive. You still think "high". It's the most natural trap in the world to fall into.

The idea of "high" notes as mythological monsters is just that, a myth.

But for those that believe in the myth it can be a bad dream that won't go away. Its only purpose is to bug you... if you or your teacher allow it to. And the more you cringe when approaching such a note, the more you will close up.

━━━━━━━

Wow! Your B naturals are beginning to knock the walls down! Even though they're still hard and brassy, you're beginning to assume some control over them.

Acc.

(sotto voce) Well, he did it to you again... they weren't B naturals.

Sopra.

I knew it! It didn't quite feel right... and you never fumble on the piano unless you take it up... how many notes?

Acc.

Just a half note... to C natural.

Everything's getting a lot easier for you. You used to sweat blood doing this in the original. Your Musetta has come a long way.

What are we going to do?

Sopra.

Today we're going to do Cherubino, and "Now at Last is the Moment "from the Marriage of Figaro… Susanna's aria. I'm trying out for both parts.

In English, Italian, or Pomeranian?

Sopra.

In English!

Oh, In English! Then I presume I shall have no problems in understanding the consonants, the vowels, and the frequency of pitch involved? Who's the pilot in command here?

Sopra.

I am!

Who's this bummer caressing the piano?

Sopra.

He's my co-pilot.

Right! It takes a helluva lot to be a good accompanist, it's a symbiotic relationship. But when your co-pilot is forced to take over … you know you are in trouble! He'll do whatever he can to tide you through… but you're the one who has to reevaluate the situation and reassume your authority.

No one else can do it for you!

———————————

Whatever vocal category you may be heir to, I don't ever want you guys to limit your vocal resources. I want you to imagine your instruments as being capable of doing justice to anything within the confines of your tessitura.

Hell, I used to sing along with all the basses, baritones, tenors, and, yes, the sopranos too!

Of course, I don't have to tell you… the coloraturas gave me a hard time.

Well, since you weren't around a century or two earlier, I guess Bellini didn't have you in mind when he wrote Sonnambula. Who knows?

He might have tried to accommodate you a little better.

I want you to tackle everything! You never know what the hell you can do until you try it! At least half the stuff you're singing now, you didn't like at all to begin with.

The only way to get better is to do the stuff you can't do!

Hell, any one can sing country music.

Sopra.

Well… you stopped me. I must be doing something wrong!

No, your "Ah non Giunge "is going rather well, but just because each and every phrase in this aria is short and sweet does not mean you also have to come to a halt at the end of each one.

This song is really just an acrobatic recitativo, but even a recitativo must have a sense of continuity. Think of each phrase as being a link in a chain.

Don't break the chain.

Okay, we'll do that all over again, it's getting easier for you.

Sopra.

Do you call it easy to transpose it right into the "passaggio"?

Passaggio? That's another garbage term. I know of at least two tenors that damned near strangled to death trying to keep an "open" throat when they had to sing an F sharp or a G. Why! Because they thought they had to use a whole different set of rules or technique to accommodate the imaginary transition from their "chest register "to their "head register ".

Why create a problem that doesn't exist… much less give a name to it? Forget about it! All it does is add to the confusion.

Oh, one more thing. Any "teacher" promoting such nonsense, I don't care how world famous… is full of crap!

Sopra.

I stopped because I didn't know if I sang the correct pitch or not… my voice feels in a different place from where it was the last time I did this.

No… I don't think your placement is any different now than what it was in the beginning of this lesson.

Sopra.

It feels lower.

Your voice is sounding a little more resonant, a little bit bigger, and much further out than it has ever been. Everything is combining to make you feel a lot freer than you used to be. You have more going for you now than you've ever had before. Revel in it!

Your "Caro Nome "still sounds a little amateurish… and that's only because a couple of your consonants, especially the M, are still a bit sluggish. You still have a tendency to linger on the M, almost but not quite, a hum. Most amateurs have this problem and they never really learn how to fix it. Don't dwell on the consonant… get on the vowel as soon as possible.

Now you know you must have your AY vowel ready, willing, and able to do its duty before you pronounce the M, so we'll just run the scales on these two words, Caro Nome.

I've never used the term octave jump before, but you understand what I'm trying to put across to you. The vowel leaps an octave above its original pitch, but these terms "leap" or "jump" encourage a subliminal sense of going "high".

In order to avoid this, all you can do under any and all circumstances is to go OUT!

A broad jump, yes… a pole vault - never!

Needless to say, it is absolutely imperative to renew the vowel on the pitch you wish to negotiate.

Sopra.

But it's not my aria... my voice isn't right for it!

Well, you're just getting warmed up and tuned in. You can sing this aria as well as any other soprano, but your voice is not spinning enough to do it justice. If this were a Verdi aria, you'd be home free. When your instrument acquires more of the sympathetic vibrations necessary to convey the limpid quality this song needs, then you'll love it!

This song demands charm... not voice. Who else but Pepe Le Pew...

that Bon Vivant Bon-Bon, has the self-assured belief that he is, indeed, God's Greatest Gift to the female gender.

He has, without a doubt, not only a truckload of charm, but also, all the attributes necessary to pursue and gain his objective.

Just pretend that you... are Pepe Le Pew!

———

That's very nice, but you didn't have to do anything for it!

Your D flat was freer and more open a few minutes ago! It was free when you thought you were only singing B flats, but you were really singing D flats!

I had brought you up a minor third... and you weren't even aware of it.

Sopra.

A whole third? Why couldn't I tell the difference?

I conned you. I just ran my thumb up and down the keyboard to distract you. That way, I screwed up your sense of relative pitch.

Sopra.

You mean to say that whole time, I was really singing D flats?

That's right. When you know you have to sing a D flat, you get shook...

you bug yourself! So all I did was give you the impression you weren't. You no longer have a fear of B flats... so what you thought was only a B flat...

was really a D flat!

I did the same thing with you last week. You thought you were singing "Caro Nome "in the original key... yes, I know... I'm sneaky.

Sopra.

Pete, I keep feeling sort of like… there's a brake screeching to a halt in my throat when I go up high… is that a bad sign?

You are not going up high! No sign at this stage of your game is bad, it's all working for you.

Sopra.

I'm not stretching my vocal cords irreparably?

No, you are not stretching anything; there's no way you can stretch your vocal cords because you are singing correctly.

It's only when you attempt to attack the upper part of your tessitura incorrectly while you are delivering that the throat muscles become "squeezed" and take the punishment, the "pressing" out on the larynx.

Of course your larynx not only has to endure these muscular constrictions, it's also being blown on by too much air charging through its domain.

After a while… I don't know whether the larynx takes a "set", collapses, or just plain throws in the sponge, but when you HAVE a "lowering" of the voice, technically, your larynx has taken so much upon itself, it just resists any further efforts on your part to get that note that was always yours before…

it can't cope anymore.

Sopra.

Why does it feel like brakes are screeching?

God knows! Maybe you got bit by a bedbug!

… in some ways, you still have the same emotional instrument mentality you had a year or so ago that you filled with all sorts of death wishes… your larynx remembers, and it still has some of the old habit patterns which we are trying to shake off.

Now, since it can take over a year for your subconscious to permanently penetrate and re-instruct the muscles of your instrument to obey your will, your larynx in the meantime is being pulled to and fro between old patterns and new ones… but, it's being pulled in the right direction.

Okay, back to square one… where the hell were we?

Well, I must admit that the lower part of your tessitura is beginning to sound a helluva lot more resplendent, it almost seems to want to assert itself! When that happens you know you're making progress. Now you tell me… above and beyond anything you feel, hope for, or imagine to be happening in the upper part of your tessitura, what is the first sign of improvement in that area?

Sopra.

Improvement in the lower part!

Right! You've known from the first lesson onward, that there's no way in hell you could do anything to improve the middle and lower parts of your voice until the upper part of your tessitura became stronger and more proficient.

There's no way in hell you can build a voice from the bottom up!

That's a prime reason why bassos don't have good E's and F's!

They keep sinking into the muck and mire. That's from the school of voice building that says the voice has to build a solid enough foundation to which we can "anchor" all the higher notes.

This not only sounds plausible to the student, but it makes the teacher a builder by proxy!

All we can do about the lower part of your voice is to leave it alone, let it sort of tag along… it'll get better. Just talk to me!

―――――――――

Ah ha… everything was fine until the last moment.

You got the E flat, but you also destroyed it in the process.

I know it's not secure enough mentally and physically in your instrument to be taken for granted yet, but you threw it all away at at the last moment, you balked!… you let your stomach do your thinking for you.

Now you know why a coward dies a thousand deaths.

Sopra.

Because his stomach does his thinking for him!

Right… if you have to go down… go down swinging!

Sopra.

You know what's happening, Pete? On the top, my face, right here, it's buzzing and tickling!

Your voice is becoming darker and warmer because the center of your focus of resonance is sending out stronger vibrations, which in turn influence the quality of the vowel.

Now you remember… I said vowel, I did not say tone!

Your instrument has acquired a bit more space inside it, and somehow or other this creates a better placement in your voice.

I don't really know why… I just know it does.

Now the more your larynx opens, the more you will feel these vibrations working for you. Of course you understand, it takes time and patience to achieve any sort of a reaction from an instrument whose only desire is to hibernate!

All we can do at the moment is keep prodding it to do our bidding. Any hesitation on your part confuses the larynx… it will always take the path of least resistance and you'll always lose half of what it has to offer.

Since you're the pilot in command… you must take charge!

What happened, why did you stop? "Ah, Non Giunge "was going great.

Sopra.

I tried to do a variation… and I screwed it up!

O.K. If something like this ever happens in a performance, you just pause a moment or two… and then come in when you feel it's right. You never let the audience know you goofed. To all intents and purposes, this was the way it was originally written!

The prima donna's rule of thumb has always been… any variations she may inflict upon the populace, above and beyond what the composer had intended… they damned well better be grateful for!

This is where you find out if your accompanist is any good or not. If he can't smell when you run into trouble, and try to help you, call a taxidermist… stuff the mother!

Now what?

Sopra.

I couldn't get it! It's driving me crazy! It was wrong from the beginning… it was totally out of synch and out of place for me, I hate it! I am not a colora-tura soprano, I am a lyrico spinto!

That doesn't make a damned bit of difference… all sopranos are coloratura sopranos! Bar none! Now you know why the big soprano voices like yours that can tackle the coloratura repertoire are so few and far between.

Their teachers don't dare encourage them to explore anything beyond the standard high C's they may be able to negotiate.

These bastards are playing safe! They haven't a clue as to how to train singers in the whys and wherefores.

"Ah, Non Giunge "may be a lot more difficult for you than "Caro Nome "was, but it's still a relatively easy aria. You're making mountains out of molehills. If it didn't have the E flat at the end of it, every soprano in captivity would be singing it!

Technically you're doing everything right, but subconsciously… you have this tendency to balk just before diving off the springboard You've got the E flat… you just don't trust it to be there.

I remember this somewhat informal get-together staged by a tenor and some of his vocal students as a display of his teaching prowess.

Of the half dozen who participated, I never forgot the one mezzo- soprano who absolutely amazed me by her ability to run scales.

A full-bodied open voice, top to bottom. She obviously was the pearl in his oyster. So naturally, she sang the Habanera from Carmen.

I knew she was singing in French, but that's all I understood! I think I may have been the only one who didn't clap. Not once did he correct her for any transgressions with the language. I felt that this talented girl was being raped.

I came away from this debacle with a sense of sorrow.

She would never rise above her status as a chorister!

Accompanist

Don't worry about it, everyone has their own physical problems to overcome. You're lucky in some ways and I'm lucky in other ways.

Sopra.

I'm lucky? What's my problem then?

Acc.

Because you can't hear yourself when you sing... no one really can...

or you can't hear anyone else when you sing and you never have really been able to.

That's why people like "H" are always upset, because they can hear other people... but that's both good fortune and misfortune. It has nothing to do with your ear... that's the way your body works.

What it means is that you've got such a big voice you can't really hear others when you sing.

Sopra.

Oh, I thought I just didn't have her musical sophistication.

Acc.

No. Why do you think it is that the teachers you studied with thought there was something wrong with your ears? They can't understand your physical problems and you cannot understand their reactions.

Sopra.

Oh, I see. My voice is so big it drowns other people out for me.

Acc.

Yes. That's why I sometimes get annoyed at you because you can't hear anything I say while you are singing. You seem to be ignoring my instructions, but that's just the way your voice works in your body.

Sopra.

Ah, it really frustrates me and I get angry at you because you keep trying to talk to me when I'm singing, and I can't hear a damned thing you're saying.

Acc.

A lot of people can hear when someone says something to them while they are singing. I don't know if all people with big voices have the same problem, but it's the way your own voice works so you will just have to learn how to make the best of it.

In some ways it doesn't matter.

Sopra.

Why?

Acc.

It's part of the quality of your voice. You wouldn't have the same voice if you could listen the way other people do.

Sopra.

So it has nothing to do with brain-ear coordination... I always thought it was a defect in my mental or musical ability.

Acc.

It's like when you go flat sometimes, it's a factor of this kind of voice you have and in the way it works in your body and it's nothing for you to feel "wrong" about. You simply have to learn how to adjust your body so it doesn't do that. It's not something anyone can teach you how to do beyond a certain point.

Sopra.

Then how can you be a good singer in trios and stuff if you can't hear what other people are doing?

Acc.

Well, no one can once they really learn how to sing; I can't hear what people are doing when I'm singing in a trio... really.

But in a way you're lucky because you had that working for you from the beginning.

Now if "H" ever learns how to sing properly, she will have some of the same problems you do because her voice will start getting bigger… and when your voice gets bigger… you have growing pains, and you have a hard time adjusting to it.

Acc.

Now if your voice doesn't grow and get bigger, you get used to it and know how to cope with it.

Now if your voice was the same as six months ago, you would never sing flat… you would know how to deal with it.

Sopra.

Oh… you mean it just remains the same.

Acc.

Right, but because it's changing, that's why you keep having to learn how to sing over and over again.

Sopra.

Well, that seems to make sense, and it also makes me feel better because all this time I felt I must be stupid or crazy in trying to learn to sing. Maybe that is why also when you make a mistake in the accompaniment that causes me to go off, I think it's my fault.

Acc.

Yes, because you can't always tell when you are right…

Sopra.

Pete, you must have taken this music up a note or two because I was able to do it at home... but the way I'm producing my voice now, it won't move.

Your instrument has changed, honey...

Sopra.

From an hour ago?

You bet your boots!

Sopra.

It was moving an hour ago before I came here!

Hang on. I hear something in your voice that's warmer and darker.

Sopra.

But its lost its agility.

Only temporarily.

Sopra.

But it won't go high anymore.

High? No such thing. The upper part of your tessitura.

Sopra.

It won't go there anymore then!

It will. There's nothing wrong with your instrument. It has changed within itself slightly to assume a new configuration. Your voice seems to have picked up a little more color or sympathetic vibrations and it's starting to turn over a little more.

Your instrument is doing the best it can for you at the moment.

As far as the upper part of your tessitura is concerned, some one else would call it a lowering of the voice. It is not!

This new configuration of the muscles within your larynx takes time to meld... so until it decides to go along with the demands you make upon it, don't chastise yourself... it isn't your fault!

All you can do is give it your best shot... let's try again.

Well, you did a lot better than you thought you could, in spite of a memory lapse.

Sopra.

I feel really offensive when I sing wrong notes or sing flat. I can't hear anything I'm doing…

How many lessons have you had? Not all that much!

Sopra.

I think I've had a lot for someone who's so dumb.

Hey, this other teacher of yours let you get away with murder!

Sopra.

She was always correcting me, always correcting my ear…

Accompanist.

That doesn't matter. She let you get by with a bad attitude, you never performed even once….

Sopra.

Then why do you keep having the impulse to correct me when I'm singing the notes? It must be because I'm singing them wrong.

Acc.

Cause you're not covering up! You have to invent the music when you get into a spot. They don't care about Verdi, they care about you.

Yeah, absolutely. Do something, even if it's wrong! That's what he's trying to get across to you….

Acc.

You couldn't ever be a singer with that attitude… you could have the most wonderful voice in the universe, and it wouldn't matter if you got up there and couldn't perform…

Sopra.

It's not my voice, I felt my voice coming out fine, it's my brain, my brain disintegrated.

Acc.

That's 'cause you let it disintegrate.

What you did was revert... like this stupid driver in front of me on the freeway. This big truck came up alongside her and instead of stepping on the gas she stepped on the brake and hunched over the wheel. I slam-dunked my brakes and honked my horn and all she did was hunch over some more and slow all the way down to almost a dead stop. The wrong thing to do. She panicked and folded into herself.   Acc.

Well, I think you are particularly bad when you have an audience, and that's wrong, you should be better when you have an audience. When you learn how to sing, you should learn how to perform. And it doesn't matter that there are a lot of assholes out there that don't know when some one's being properly trained, or when they're not being properly trained.

They can't even tell when some one's singing well or not.

Sopra.

What I just did was terrible, I blurred all the scales.

Say Bill, did you take this music down half a note?

Acc.

No, I played everything in the correct key.

Well that explains everything… your voice is lower, that's why you hear it different, your voice is lower.

I also thought it sounded like the song was a half note lower in pitch than it sounded like when you did it before.

That's great for your team because your voice is now fuller and more resonant than it has ever been and that's also why you have problems with the D up there. Your instrument wants to close or cut off on the C and C# a bit because it hasn't quite melded and is still trying to adjust itself… so naturally your D is going to suffer.

Sopra.

Will I get it back?

Naturally! My God… you didn't have a B, C, or D a year ago when we first started, don't fuss… all the notes in the upper part of your tessitura may come and go… but they will always come back bigger and stronger and more secure all the time. They may grumble or get balky… but they have no choice in the matter.

You don't have any choice in the matter either! You work with what you got. But now you've got a freer and a more open instrument. That's all we can hope for at this stage of the game.

Back to work!

[Pete, perhaps you'd better explain: when the voice gains in size and color, it can temporarily lose agility and some of its upper range - but if the singer keeps trusting and singing correctly, the new voice will loosen up and regain the lost notes and coloratura.

Think of a pair of dancing shoes and a young dancer whose feet are growing - when her shoes begin to pinch, the dancer will be less graceful - until she gets a new pair of shoes. When the voice is comfortable with its new size and strength it will leap higher and dance more gracefully than ever.]

(No dancer whose feet were still growing would think of binding them , Chinese-fashion, to stop their growth!)

Your oppressed proofer J.A.

All right... I'll go along with this...

Well... it's taken a long time, but this aria is beginning to sound like it's got something going for it, not bad at all.

Sopra.

I like it well enough, but I don't think I'm constituted to do it justice.

Justice! Hell, you sing this aria better than anybody. Don't be so hard on yourself. You're too conscientious. Do you honestly believe even half the singers you have ever heard did justice to the composer? Hell no! Even the composer himself understood that a day never goes by without someone, somewhere, screwing up his music.

As long as his music is being sung or played, why should he grumble about it? He's achicving immortality!

Anytime you lose trust in what you are doing, you will subconsciously wrap yourself up in a cocoon. That's how psychiatrists make fortunes. You've got claws! Use them!

"Sombre Foret "may be in French, but don't get subtle with the language, just keep using your Italianate vowels.

In this aria you're only speaking in the lower part of your tessitura, and you don't have to do anything, or change anything even when you're on the A flats or A naturals. Screw that "passaggio" crap! Don't make a big deal out of it.

As far as you're concerned, an A natural is only in the middle part of your voice.

Talk to me!

Sopra.

I'm not getting up there...

You are listening too hard to yourself... you're getting all wrapped up in it, you're not talking to an audience, you're talking to yourself. Here... talk to this teddy bear. He's a good listener.

Sopra.

But I can't find the notes...

You have a new instrument, a new voice... it's going to feel strange to you until you become accustomed to it.

Sopra.

It sounds inside my head like it's really plain and straight... not turning over at all...

It's turning over all right, your voice sounds warmer, bigger and more easily produced. It's like anything else that's new to you, that's unfamiliar... it takes a little time getting used to it. Don't bug yourself, bug the audience... that's what they're paying you for!

Sopra.

To bug them?

Yes! They came to hear you insult them!

Sopra.

Oh... all right... if they paid good money for their tickets, with a voice like mine, I could always do that!

(If you can't do anything else with a soprano who's shook out of shape - make her laugh.)

Sopra.

There's something wrong, I can feel it. I'm back to where I started a year ago. It's all very thin and screechy. After I sang Non Mi Dir in my last lesson, I lost all my coloratura. I've been damaged ever since.

I didn't quite realize the extent of the vocal change you've been going through. So far, yours have usually lasted about a week, just long enough to confuse you. But this one is a major change.

It is not thin, it is not screechy. Your voice is bigger and more resonant than ever before. Hell, you're just getting warmed up!

Your instrument took about three weeks to adjust itself, meld itself, heal up… call it anything you want. You haven't lost anything at all… you're just hearing your voice in an entirely different way than you have ever heard it before!

You have to realize, in your new voice you've got a new partner to work with. He's going to be a lot more amiable, than your old one.

Give yourself a little time to get acquainted with him!

You'll get along just fine.

━━━━━━

You're under, you are not flat… you are just under the pitch.

You are under because you are trying to hear the piano, hear the baritone, and also hear yourself. You are trying to blend. Whenever you try to accommodate any one, or make allowances, your voice will suffer.

You cannot ever minimize what you have to work with.

To hell with the baritone, to hell with the pianist, to hell with the chorus. They are concerned only with what they are doing!

The only one you pay attention to is the conductor. He's presumed to be the one in charge… let him get it all together!

If he isn't aware of what the hell is going on… you take charge!

Pay attention to what you know to be right, and what you must do to achieve it.

Even in the quartet from Rigoletto, every one's singing solo.

━━━━━━

Oh my… you just sang that whole phrase a minor third above the original… you took an E flat above C!

Sopra.

I what… an E flat? Did you do that on purpose or did I just get screwed up?

You got screwed up. But what you just did was stay in the same place…

you took a chance, you believed in what you were doing, there was no hesitation.

Sopra.

I had no idea of what I was doing.

Right! All you really did was "parlate"… you spoke, right?

The E flat in your voice sprung forth only because you had no fear of it. Now you trusted the C in your voice to be there, right?… and God knows you don't always do that… but this time everything worked the way it's supposed to. You're going to have a helluvan E some day.

Sopra.

When I auditioned for that conductor in Oakland, he thought a D was too high for me…

He's like the rest of those (expletive deleted) who think they know something about voice… they can't hear the inherent potential of a voice, they only hear what they think is the finished product.

They can't explain anything either… they can only criticize.

Sopra.

He also teaches!

Well… all conductors coach.

Sopra.

No. He teaches voice!

Oh my God!

 rò,   mo - - - - ri - rò!

The famous last word in Leonara's "Tacea la Notte" from Trovatore, simplified for the student as shown.

Mirirò is one word. I want a moe, a ree, and a row, row, row your boat. Moe will give you the E flat, ree will cling to the E flat and since row knows where he belongs, he will ascend to the A flat, without any conscious effort on your part.

As soon as you think you have to go somewhere or do something to "get" the A flat, you will automatically increase any apprehension you may have and this will involuntarily affect your instrument.

Because we had ran "moriro" through two octaves up and down the great scale to get the pattern and the feel for this word, that does not mean this word is going to feel comfortable on another series of pitches. In order for this aria to finish in a manner that will give the audience a sense of security, not to mention yourself, the "moe" vowel on the E flat must be renewed for six beats, the "ree" vowel on the E flat held for one beat, and the "row" vowel on the A flat renewed till the end of time!

This is what technique is all about.

Every consonant, every vowel, and every word has to be planned, plotted, and premeditated to form a mental and physical pattern that you can depend upon to deliver your message.

Sopra.

I kept losing my voice...

No, you thought you were, but you weren't. We're putting a tremendous amount of pressure on your instrument, you have to understand that. You're on the verge of crossing another barrier.

Because we're doing this aria up two half tones, your voice will naturally get balkier... it's not used to it. You don't have to do this song justice or anything... we're just using it to work with.

You might say we're right up against this barrier now. We're chipping away with a genteel sledge hammer, but it still won't budge, we still haven't broken free.

Now your voice is going because you demand it to go; we're not coaxing it to comply like we usually do.

You might say we're dragging it along, like a dog on a leash.

Sooner or later, it has to give up. We're going beyond its capacity to resist... we're gonna give it a nervous breakdown.

It's the only way to free up your instrument; nothing else works

---

We're going to finish your lesson with a new approach. Since you know Tacea la Notte this well now, I want you to perform this song as if you can't go wrong. Therefore, thou shalt inform each and every member of the audience... that this aria is for you, and you alone.

How? I want you to sing only the one word... You.

Sopra.

You want me to sing Tacea La Notte on the OO vowel only...

Not quite. Because the word you has a Y in it, this word will subconsciously prevent your tongue from rising any more than it has to and this vowel seems to cater to your voice, so let's put it to work!

One thing more... don't SING anything... just recite it.

So you failed an audition… big deal! You auditioned for these people just to find out what you and your voice could accomplish. Well, you found out!

" Tacea La Notte "isn't all that easy to sing, but at least you have reached the stage wherein you feel you are good enough to audition, that's something!

One thing more. Those that sit in judgement on you aren't always that knowledgeable! I'm not knocking them, but don't ever give any one judging your voice credit for knowing too much!

Most singers - even famous ones - would have quit before the finish line if they had felt that way!

Just as in any beauty contest, each judge compares each girl to his own preconceived heart's delight.

While I won't deny there are those who may be quite objective in their opinions, I still maintain there are just as many that are in essence, only pretending to be. Even great maestros can let their emotions cloud their judgement.

If Iva Pacetti had listened to Toscannini, the world would have lost a great soprano.

Sopra.

It's not working. Everything is so loud in this room, the piano, the echoes, that I can't hear myself. I don't know what I'm doing. How can I follow the accompanist and keep correct time?

You're following the accompanist?

Sopra.

Yes. I can't hear how fast he's going. He taught me how to do this, I have to follow him! When I can't hear him, I think I must be out of tune!

Wait a moment. You've memorized this song, right? You know this song, right? What the hell do you need him for? He's there to accompany you!

You do whatever the hell you want with it! You are not there to accompany him. As long as he thinks you are in charge of what you're doing… he will follow you like a good puppy dog!

You're the pilot in command… fly the airplane!

I once arrived at an important audition with just enough time to put down my workman's tools and stride on stage.

Several of the auditioners (dressed in their sunday best) could hardly believe their eyes.

Having no choice in the matter, I was wearing a pair of scruffy blue coveralls and also looked a little disheveled in the bargain.

Having nothing to lose, I never sang better in my life!

No, I wasn't what they were looking for, but I learned something.

If I had sounded or sung as well as Richard Crooks, I could have looked like a bag bum with a pushcart... they would want me!

Are you male or female?

Sopra.

Female!

O.K., that I'll take for granted, anything else is up for grabs. When in Rome, you are a Roman... in Buzzards Bay, that's in Mass.... you're a buzzard!

Since Manon is French Catholic, you are French Catholic. If Manon was a Jewish princess... then you're a Jewish princess!

Like a chameleon, you must be able to assume the identity of the character you are portraying... whatever it takes. You disregard all religious, social, political or whatever... beliefs you may have. You don't take them on stage with you... leave them in the dressing room.

Now, you and I both know, that Casta Diva does not belong to you yet... someday it will! All in all, you did sing it much better than you thought you did, otherwise, I would have stopped you.

Callas made you believe she was Norma... that's what I'm trying to say.

Now Norma may be a Druid priestess, but there's nothing chaste about her... she's a sexpot! Just put more "pussy" into it!

Sopra.

Cigna said "Casta Diva "was a meditation, not a big dramatic aria.

That's true, but only the words are meditative. If you prostrate your persona, your voice and your body to a higher authority… you'll have nothing left to work with! You cannot ever allow whatever message you may be delivering to interfere with and override your natural instincts for survival. You'll go down with the ship!

Vibrations do not meditate! Allow them to propagate! Comprende?

———————

I can't stand it anymore… you're going lower than I can!

Sopra.

Where did I go?

Acc.

Just to the basso low C…

Sopra.

Was I audible down there?

Acc.

Every word… I've never heard a mezzo sing this low.

You were not singing in the bass tessitura. What you were doing was "speaking on pitch "in the basso tessitura. You've come to the point wherein you have proved to yourself you can do it. The only reason the lower part of your tessitura is this good is because the upper part of your voice is so much more open and free. Right?

Your instrument has nothing to do with anything, it's your intelligence.

Just because your instrument can go by itself you don't take anything for granted. Just zero in on what you're doing.

Sopra.

I think my placement is changing, because I can't feel anymore what note I'm on as exactly as I used to...

You have a feeling of disorientation, is that it?

From a technical viewpoint, all you can do is to articulate; pronounce; know what you have to do with the vowel; open your nasal passages; allow no negative thoughts to propagate; stand and deliver; do what you know to be right... and perhaps it may coax your sense of placement back to where you feel it belongs.

You know what's evolving and why. Your sense of placement at this moment is not strong enough to override the physical changes occurring in your instrument.

All you can do is to ride it out. Let the chipmunks fall where they may!

Hang on...

Sopra.

Am I doing this wrong again?

No... you were perfect until you came to the octave jump, then you opened your mouth more than you had to. What is it... G to G?

Acc.

B flat to B flat.

You mean you were singing B flats what you just did now?

Sopra.

Yeah.

I forgive you. They sounded so low... they fooled me completely. You didn't brace for the B flat, you didn't lunge for the B flat, you trusted the B flat to be there... and it was.

(This is very embarrassing... I thought I was omnipotent)

Even a good coloratura can hardly vocalize to an A natural above C…

why the wry face?

Sopra.

I heard the tape of my last lesson.

So?

Sopra.

You've always had me going for quantity… see how big a range… see how much power… because it was impossible that a voice like mine could ever sound beautiful or charming… so we went for quantity instead of quality.

You've got the same kind of instrument to work with as Maria Callas had. She wasn't ashamed to be known as the girl with the big ugly voice. She didn't have anything more to work with than you have.

But her indomitable sense of purpose always strove to ferret out something she could believe in, some measure of truth in what she was doing. She was not one to believe in pipe dreams.

She didn't waste time wishing her natural voice had been prettier than it was when she started.

There's a helluva lot of beautiful voices out there that will never achieve even half of their true potential. Damned near most of them could never hope to fill a theatre without a microphone… much less sing anything at all in the original key.

The true quality or beauty of any voice only becomes evident when the instrument is fully developed and functioning correctly.

By my yardstick, this comes out to be about one in two hundred.

Rest assured, you're one of the two hundred!

Have you got claws?

Sopra.

Yes!

In the wild, survival demands you kill! No one else is going to feed you. The way you minced your way through this song, you could starve to death. You're so elegant, the mouse that roared could take a bone away from you.

Go for the jugular! I want you to rend, to relish... to taste blood!

Sopra.

Ooouuu...

No ooouuus, Callas always tasted blood! She had the killer instinct. In the service, the first sergeant's prime directive is to instill discipline. Well, that's what you've got... but, in order to survive, if you haven't got the killer instinct, it has to be honed, implanted in some way.

Just imagine yourself to be the green eyed dragon with the thirteen tails... so beware... take care... I'm hungry!

"Suicidio" demands more than your voice is capable of giving at this stage of the game. Someday, it will belong to you, but at this moment you are working with a Lucia instrument. There's a lot of pain, a lot of angoscia in Gioconda... right? Together, with her courage, that's what makes her what she is. It's a killer role.

"Suicidio" demands this angoscia, but it also demands some very lyrical passages. Compromise. You don't have to knock the walls down. I don't want you to whomp your voice around, otherwise you are going to need more than a band-aid to heal yourself afterwards.

I know that "Suicidio" is a complete change of pace for you, and it will take its toll, but you know enough now not to bear down or to deliberately try to darken the lower part of your tessitura. I know that makes a good effect, but it's not natural, and also very dangerous to the instrument.

Lighten it up a bit. How about "Oy, vey!" instead of "Suicidio"?

Acc.

Her voice has a much more spinto sound than it did a week ago, without being heavy and pressed sounding.

You're right! It's spinning, and it's big and warm, even though that the instrument is off.

Sopra.

My instrument is off? Could you explain that to me? What's off about it?

Acc.

Your placement is different. It's getting better.

Sopra.

Yes, that's it! I felt my high C to be where my G is. It felt lower.

What you're doing now, is singing with half... half of what you've got coming into your voice! The other half ain't there yet!

Maybe Monday, Tuesday, Thursday... who knows? At this stage of the game, only you, me, or your accompanist, could sense your voice to be a little out of whack.

Don't fuss over it, you're not responsible for anything.

Sopra.

Well, I guess that Meyerbeer concert I gave, really did help my voice.

—————

A world famous soprano became so immersed in doing justice to her role in a Wagnerian opera: the acting, the stagecraft, the interpretive nuances, etc. that she was forced to take a year off, to recuperate from the after-effects!

That's above and beyond the call of duty.

As conscientious as you may be about what you're doing musically and dramatically, don't ever take your voice for granted.

The survival of your instrument is your prime directive.

Nothing else matters! Thou shalt never sacrifice thy voice, for any reason whatsoever, upon the altar of "Art".

Alright, you know we're working your instrument to get out of it the ultimate it has to offer. Leonora's aria is the toughest thing you've tried to sing so far. Some parts sound big and metallic, and the rest sounds warm and hard... it's a mixed bag. In a year or so, this aria will belong to you, but right now it's taking its toll on your instrument.

Sopra.

You're always giving me something new and more difficult to sing... why can't you let me sing something easier and more comfortable for a change?

Ah, ha, that's what the rest of these bastards do. You've gone way beyond what your former teachers ever hoped to accomplish with what you had to work with. They let you sing what you thought you could do justice to, what they felt was easy for you, what sounded good in your voice... how the hell could you make any progress?

You know now that these incompetent miscreants were running an emotional catering service, physically recycling not only their old garbage, over and over again... but yours too!

What I'm going after is what your voice is capable of achieving, not what you can do right now with your voice!

They're two different things.

═══════════════

Sopra.

Pete, I'm cracking on C's now...

You didn't trust where you were going, what did you expect? If you didn't know this scale, I'd understand, but I can hear you listening to and verifying every note you're singing going up this scale. You can't help but lose your forward momentum.

If your vowel wasn't as good as it is, you would have lost everything much sooner. You don't watch what your feet are doing climbing stairs, you just go ahead and do it.

The most important vowel in this scale is the one you are going to end up on, that's the one you're aiming for!

Sopra.

I just don't think I'll ever get it right... it sounds terrible.

Don't fret about it. Just because you weren't born with the ability to bob your instrument up and down only means you're going to have to work that much harder. I don't know too much about it either. You're the only soprano I've ever taught that had any interest whatsoever in learning how to trill. Today it's almost a lost art.

Sopra.

It's just so frustrating.

Well, so far you've managed to move it out a lot better this lesson. Of course its not vibrating at the speed of light but at least you've come to the point wherein the vowel a half step above your dominant vowel is beginning to clean up its act. They both sound clean and clear.

I remember reading something when I was a student that the French school was just about the last holdout in making the trill or the shake a mandatory part of their training. They forced their students to go way beyond what they were willing to settle for.

You're going to have to do the same thing.

Oh yeah. I don't know if talking to another soprano would do you any good... my guess is that they'll either bluff their way through it, or change the subject.

Sopra.

It's a mess… it feels completely out of tune… what happened?

We brought the music up half a note, I felt it would be easier for you… more comfortable in the upper part of your tessitura.

Sopra.

Ooohhh… It just feels all wrong and out of place…

Whoa… there's nothing to panic about. You feel the change now, right? That's great! You now have a feeling of placement, of where everything belongs.

You get this funny kind of a feeling when something is wrong. It's really weird. Whenever some one pulls this kind of con on you, usually out of malice, you'll know how to cope with it.

Sopra.

They will do that… play the music higher than it is written?

Yep! I was in this fancy bar where they featured operatic entertainment and had their own stable of singers. I was asked to sing. In the intro to "Core Ingrato ", the accordion player got real fancy. As soon as I started to sing I knew something was wrong, but I had no idea of what the hell it could be. Now it's a question of sink or swim. I did what I knew I had to do and my sense of placement stayed with me. I didn't know until much later what really happened.

A friend of mine told me the accordionist played everything a half tone higher. The s.o.b. was hoping I'd crack on the B natural.

Now you're getting a feeling of placement, where everything belongs. That's what you've been been working for, these last couple of years.

===========

Nowadays, anything more than two octaves is considered exemplary.

I have no objection whatsoever to you filling in for the basso at the rehearsal. Hell, sing everything you can handle.

Your low F may even be better than his… but, I don't think anyone would put a coloratura spinto to work singing Sparafucile!

Sopra.

Pete, I'm getting really tight. My throat's getting tight, my jaw's getting tight, under my chin is really tight… why is this happening?

Why? I don't really know. I know your voice has opened up, your instrument. You sound wide open, you're forward, and your voice is spinning like crazy.

I think you're getting too apprehensive about doing justice to Lucia's quakes and quivers. It's like flying over water. Every time I've flown over water the engine has never failed to sound a helluva lot rougher. As soon as I'm over land again it's absolutely amazing how the engine will now settle down and smooth itself out.

Does the airplane know it's over water? Nope. Who does? I do!

Sopra.

But Pete… you know what? I feel better when it's over water… because I can swim.

(Oh boy… female logic)

======================

Hell, everybody in the world would be the greatest singer in the world, if their instrument, their larynx, obeyed their emotions… but they haven't trained it that way.

Clinically speaking, your vocal apparatus is just another collection of body parts that must be trained to work in harmony.

Now, emotionally you could have done what you're doing now, after these past few years, at the first lesson you ever had, but your instrument wouldn't have obeyed you. Now, you can almost throw technique away, because your instrument goes for you.

But… you don't ever want to…

The better your physical instrument becomes, the greater the temptation to indulge in vocal pyrotechnics… so, unless you keep a very tight rein on how and what you are doing… your emotions will also cut your throat!

That's what happened to Callas… her tempestuous nature overrode her physical resources and tore her voice to shreds…

No singer can afford to have that happen.

Sopra.

I've still got the same problems I've always had with this aria, I'm singing the same notes flat, I'm distorting the same vowels, I'm running out of air…

You're not moving out, you're dwelling on Leonora's misfortunes, her angst, her miseria. Just because you assume the identity of some one whose emotions are in a turmoil does not mean you have to inflict turmoil upon yourself!

No way! That's the best way in the world to tear your voice apart.

It destroys the spontaneity, the vitality that impels your instrument to deliver.

I know it's a bit of a paradox, but just consider how many times people lie .. with sincerity! They subdue whatever they may really feel, in order to gain an advantage. You don't actually have to feel the character's emotions, all you have to do is make the audience feel them! Under no circumstances do you ever malign your voice in this manner.

Now Canio, in Pagliacci, may be laughing on the outside and crying on the inside… but in order to deliver, and to salvage your voice, you have to laugh on the inside… and cry on the outside.

Let the orchestra supply the turmoil, you just supply the voice!

―――――――――

Turandot's aria "In Questa Reggia", only goes to a C natural.

It's a verismo piece of music very few sopranos are capable of doing justice to. Your voice is big enough to handle it. In its own way the aria is very melodic. What I want you to do is to consider it as pure recitativo. Don't give any more than you've got to work with! In order to forestall any apprehensions of the stress and strains you may feel forthcoming―-and you will―-I want you to imagine you are now in the opera house. An opera house coach has heard all the symptoms of a voice not tuned in, not warmed up, out of whack, or what have you. His job is to teach you the musical values of your part, not to subject you or your vocal technique to undue criticism.

Your job is to memorize his musical comments and apply them.

What you sound like doesn't matter, you work with what you've got.

You're on your own… just try to conserve your resources, and as long as you remember to SPEAK the aria, you'll never give more than you should, you'll never force.

I will say it again… interpretation is also subconscious!

Anytime Callas sang you knew damn well 90 % of her brains were working overtime.

You haven't really lost anything yet, but in another few minutes you would have lost about 10 % of what you have to work with.

Your voice would then assume a kind of "cloudy" quality. You'll get through the aria alright, but that isn't good enough!

You're letting 90% of your voice take over and you're only using 10 % of your brains! You can get away with it because your voice has reached this stage of improvement. All singers fall into this trap! Singers forget the process wherein they learned how to sing in the first place and begin to rely upon their voice to do the right thing. They begin to take their voice for granted.

The more Mother Nature has given to you, the more likely it is you will run into trouble at a later date. The better you become, the easier it is to fall into bad habits.

The old cliche of singing on your interest, not your capital, really means you sing with your intelligence, not your vocal endowments!

━━━━━━━━━

Everything's working for you, you sound good… but for some reason or other, you're still plowing through the music. La Donna E Mobile is easy enough to sing because the music carries you along. It's the same with Musetta's Waltz Song. The music propels you.

Just because this aria is a lot more melancholy than the stuff you've been singing, it still has a life force of its own… and you're not tapping into it! Some songs carry you along almost like a tidal wave. This song has an ebb and a flow to it like a tide. You have to feel the surge when the music demands it. It's more of a gut instinct, than anything I can teach you. You can sing it… but you can't really put it across, you don't have the style for it right now.

I have no objection to anything you want to sing, but no one can do justice to everything. Just because you fall in love with some one does not mean you're good for each other. Let's try something else!

Let's go through this again… what did you just say?

Sopra.

I said, that I felt like I was making too big a deal of it, and that's why I wasn't getting the D's in the song like I was getting in the exercise.

What did I say?

Sopra.

You said that the instrument fades out on the D's, I can get them when I sing scales, but I can't always get them when I have to deal with vowels and consonants and regular stuff like that.

Running scales to A above "high" C only shows what this big spinto of yours is capable of. Your instrument is doing the best it can under the circumstances, but in the uppermost part of your tessitura, just about in the region of the D's and E flats, your instrument isn't strong enough yet, it hasn't got the stamina to sustain your demands.

All things considered, what you have is about 70 % of your vocal potential going for you. That's more than enough to beat all those other sopranos you used to envy. Damned near all of them were only hoping to keep what they had.

Your instrument has just about reached the point of no return.

It has to get better and better. It has no choice in the matter.

It's the only way it knows how to work!

━━━━━━━

Since Day One, the feeling of where your voice belongs has become stronger and stronger. Because of this feeling of placement, you can sense immediately anything strange or unusual happening.

Sopra.

Well, you know what? I keep losing my F above C while my D gets stronger. Then my D will get crinkly again and my F will come back… then my F will go away and my D will come back. It's really weird.

It happens to all voices. It's a balancing act.

The bigger the voice, the more conspicuous these changes are.

When you become happy with what you've got, you'll stop changing and growing, and this "problem" will disappear… but then, you'll never achieve your full potential.

You've come a long way since your first lesson. Today, no one hearing you sing would recognize your voice as being the same one they may have heard four years ago. Any one hearing you sing today would absolutely believe…

you had to be born with it.

You have reached the point wherein you know you are good enough, your standards high enough, to hold your own. You know what to do, and how to do it. All I want to impress upon you at this moment is to not get artsy-craftsy… you don't ever want to forget the process wherein you learned how to sing.

Everything you've ever learned, and everything you've ever done, has been founded on the concept that you are not singing a god-damned thing! You are merely speaking on pitch.

I know you didn't get a chance to sing as much as you would like to have done this lesson, but I felt it was more important for you to go over everything you need to know about what you've learned so far.

You must learn to recognize your mistakes, why they occurred, and, most importantly, how to correct them.

Having your teacher tell you… "that's nice"… during your whole lesson, doesn't mean you're getting any better.

In no particular order; you've learned to trust yourself more; not to chastise yourself for screwing up; to open your nose, not your mouth; that the pitch is subconscious, dependent only upon the way you form your consonants and vowels; to pay no attention to what you think you sound like; your voice has no boundaries limiting it, so you are losing the fear of going "high"… of course you can't excel in everything you want to sing… no one can… you may be temperamentally unsuited to it.

You're also learning how to improve your placement; how to make your tongue work for you; how to correct things as you go along; how to use what you've got to work with… that's enough for now… I can't remember everything either!

You're getting better only because you're working your ass off!

When you become satisfied with what you are doing and how you're doing it… when you're no longer challenged to improve yourself… when your ego takes over, then… you won't ever get any better!

There's always some stupid thing that needs to be worked on…

Baritone

The first person I ever took a voice lesson from gave me Mercutio's "Queen Mab" aria (from Gounod) to study, but I never learned it with him.

Why did he give you this aria?

Bari.

Because I was doing some French thing (Fille des Rois) that he thought was too hard for me, so he gave me this one and another one.

He gave you this… a raw-assed student that didn't have, or know anything?

Bari.

Yes. The other aria he gave me I still think is so hard that I would never do it. My second teacher gave me Athanael's "Alexandrie" aria from "Thais"… which is a real killer.

You're telling me that these two numquids gave you these arias to study… even though neither of them could sing such material themselves!

Bari.

Yes.

This reminds me of a good friend of mine… a pure lyric tenor…

whose teacher (expletives deleted) gave him "Hai Ben Raggione", that very dramatic and difficult piece from Puccini's Il Tabarro.

I told my friend that even I… who had the voice for it… couldn't do it!

He trusted my judgement and found a new teacher.

━━━━━━━━━━

Your voice tops out on the D natural. Your E flat shows no sign of ambition, and needless to say, you know your E, and everything above it… is non-existent.

Basically, you've only got one thing going for you… your tongue does come up with the pitch… but, it doesn't rise with the pitch any more than necessary.

Now voice teachers as a rule, are not going to tell you what I'm going to tell you now. You're going to have to work your ass off for about a year, more or less, for every half-note above a D natural.

This means that your instrument, your larynx, will take about a year to integrate or consolidate within itself the necessary stamina to deliver an E flat when called upon.

Of course, your D in the meantime will naturally get stronger and better placed and your E natural will begin to show signs of life.

At the end of your second year, your E natural being nurtured in this manner will also influence your F natural to propagate itself.

So, at the end of the third year, again I say more or less, you, as a baritone, should have an F natural you can depend upon.

Of course, there will be times when you will exceed these boundaries within your voice whereas you may be able to negotiate an F sharp or even a halfway decent G natural.

So, even though Mother Nature has short-changed you, with your help, she can still perform miracles.

Well, you have three vowels in your voice that seem somewhat congenial... that's the good news... the other two vowels in your instrument feel no compulsion whatsoever to behave... so that's why you feel your voice sounds hard and screechy at times.

Your AY and EE vowels don't spin.. turn over.. so they sound "squared". Now the AY and the EE are the most penetrating vowels in the human voice... the most brilliant.

I think that any one born with either of these two vowels as their dominant vowel lucked out... I know I didn't.

They also happen to be the two most difficult vowels to "fix".

Now you know your tongue comes up when you are singing either of them, but that can't be helped.

The only way to tame them, is to always assume the OH position on your lips... I know that's impossible, but it's all we can do. Just making the attempt will help you to keep from opening your mouth too wide and your lips from spreading from side to side.

I learned the hard way: The less you open your mouth, and the less you show your teeth, the more correct you are.

Here, take this cigarette. As far as you're concerned it's lit.

Now take a deep puff... and blow me a smoke ring as big as a basketball.

Good! That's your OH vowel position.

I know what I'm going to tell you now sounds ridiculous… But I can't help it. Every time you sing an R in english, you sound like Elmer Fudd! Hell, even my cat can roll a better R than you can!

But your "Some Enchanted Evening "is going to need a lot more than good intentions. Stranger is not stranguh, crowded is not cwouded, her is not huh!

So! From now on.. it doesn't make a dammed bit of difference what language you are trying to hurdle.. you are going to trill me an Italian R. I don't want that tongue of yours obeying the call of the wild!

Since we have been trying to establish some sense of placement within your voice, from now on, every scale we run I want the consonants T and D to precede all your vowels. I want you to say draw, trow, tray, tree, drew…

whatever combination you feel comfortable with.

Basso

I see. You want me to crow and grow…

I don't care if you grrrrrowl them out!

———

Whoa! "La Calunnia" may be "slander's whisper," but I don't want you to whisper or subdue anything! Your instrument isn't strong enough or proficient enough to carry this interpretive burden.

You've been to enough auditions and stuff to know that when a singer gets into trouble, all his "interpretive" skills go out the window. He just hopes to get through with the piece and survive.

Now I know you know this song. When the time comes to perform, then your gut instinct takes over… whatever you feel you may be able to play with, get away with, or subdue, fine… all well and good!

You never know what kind of shape you or your voice may be in, so all these preconceived notions of "interpretation" only serve to stifle or suppress your natural instincts to deliver.

"Celeste Aida" is a relatively straightforward aria. It's really quite simple... a melodic recitativo.

All the tenors, even today, have this insane idea you have to throw the consonant at the pitch... no you do not!

It's an old tenor trick. Hell, most of them didn't know any better. Their teachers knew even less!

Tenors, especially, are hard enough to teach, since they all have an inborn instinct to reach for the pitch, always trying to hurdle the pitch and connect up a vowel, a tone, or a consonant to it.

Their gut instinct is to "get the note" ... what happens after that is another story.

They weren't taught to anticipate articulating the consonant just prior to leaving whatever pitch or vowel they were on.

Even those that know enough to put the consonant on the vowel they are leaving screw up! They more or less "scoop" the vowel from the F to the B flat, hoping to deposit the required consonant somewhere along the route.

I'm surprised many of them lasted as long as they did.

Once a tenor begins to understand that all the consonants and all the vowels, being more or less in the same place in his voice, help him in establishing the desired pitch, that, in fact, the consonant launches the vowel, which contains the pitch, then he might begin to shake off whatever goofy notions he's been saddled with.

It sounds complicated, but it's really quite simple. When you do it that way, leaving the consonant on the F, you don't have to put it on the "high" B flat! Now you're beginning to understand why you have to put the consonant on the vowel you are leaving.

The EE vowel in your voice sounds higher than it really is, in comparison to your other vowels. Because of this, your other vowels sound larger and more resonant. If you sang this whole aria on only the EE vowel, your voice, the size of it, would seem smaller than it actually is. Your EE vowel isn't vigorous enough, it hasn't enough heft to it, to make itself more dominant. The only way to improve it, is to improve your dominant vowels. The better they become, the healthier your EE vowel becomes.

It is not ah, lui… it is Awe, Loo-Wee. Even so, your ah, lui is good enough to get by. But you're dealing with me, not your audience. It sounds good enough, but that's not good enough!

Technically you are spreading your EE vowel by stretching your lips sideways. I know, you see singers do this all the time. It's an unconscious habit they can never seem to get rid of. When you stretch your lips sideways in this manner, you lose the focus of the vowel on your lips, and your EE vowel will always sound undernourished.

In your instrument, your EE and AY vowels are the weakest. I want your AY and EE vowels to always assume the OH position.

Otherwise… you'll always be making faces at the audience!

Bari.

What about the "inner smile" some teachers talk about?

"Inner" is the key word here. "Inner" by definition, means or implies NOT OUTER. An "inner smile" is involuntary.

It's taken me years, but I now have an "inner smile" without even being aware of it. You haven't got it yet… it takes time and patience. You can't hurry its development.

It'll come in… but before it comes in… you have to do everything you can to encourage it. Just keep "sniffing" away.

═══════════

You seem to have almost no control over your reflexes.

Your body goes one way and your brains go the other!

Every time you do something wrong or think you do..you freeze up.

Even when you're singing well… you end up looking like a trapped kitten!

I know, what I'm telling you hurts. The truth about something or other always seems to hurt. If you accept it, you're on the road to recovery… if you don't, pray for a miracle!

No one else can make these decisions for you… it's up to you!

Since the Ay and EE vowels are not sympatico to your instrument, they will always have a tendency to rebel and drag their asses when called upon. These two vowels will always go along with you in the middle part of your voice, or seem to anyway, but when you demand their presence in the upper part of your tessitura, you damned well better have a good consonant to lead them forth.

Your "quella" sounds like a cross between a duck and a nanny goat. I don't want a queh vowel, I want a quay vowel... like in, which qway to Cucamonga?

After you say quay, you only suggest the first L. Then I want the second L to precede the vowel Awe. If your L is not quick enough, precise enough, quella will become two words... quehl-lah.

Don't dwell on the L!

Okay, now what are you going to hold in your hand out there?

Baritone

My nose!

That's right. When we first started, I had you hold your larynx out there in the palm of your hand. So far, so good... but your OH vowel still sounds too wooden. It needs all the facial and nasal vibrations you can conjure up. They will give your OH vowel a lot more warmth. You probably won't be able to hear them, but you damned sure will be able to feel them. One more thing...

I want your nose to be as big as the ones on Mt. Rushmore!

Your instrument, for all the mysticism attached to it, is the same as a light bulb.

Nobody in the audience, or at the audition cares how or why it works the way it does, they are only interested in the light.

No one really cares too much about the shape, the size, or the beauty of the bulb... if it doesn't light up... it's useless!

You, of course, have to know how it works... and whether your original bulb was hand-crafted by Tiffany or mass-produced matters not. Any message you must deliver is always conveyed by the spirit within you.

Light up the stage!

I want you to augment your intelligence physically. When you pick up a sword, that gives momentum to your thoughts. When you move on stage, or wherever, always try to move forward, towards someone or something. Moving in this manner increases your perceptive ability or awareness of what you are singing about. It also releases some of the subconscious tensions building up in your voice and body. It makes things easier.

Just move yourself out a little at a time… I don't expect you to hurdle tall buildings at a single bound.

"Cortigiani, vil raza, dannata" is taking too much of a toll on your instrument, you're giving too much. Rigoletto may be furious but he's not running amok! Instead of vilifying them as all Rigolettos do, I want you to question them. Cortigiani? vil raza dannata?

This will reduce a lot of the tension in your delivery, and I don't think any one could tell the difference anyhow.. one thing more:

In order to form a more perfect union between your words, your emotions, and the bond or intimacy between you and your instrument, I want you to sing this aria as a love song. Everything you will ever sing is, in its own way, a love affair between you and your voice.

Despite the urgency of the message you are delivering, you have to achieve some semblance of vocal elegance.

I know you're standing tall, but there's still too much tension in your body… here, grab this… it's a genuine Australian boomerang.

It doesn't matter what you grab hold of… you are in essence transferring whatever tensions you may generate in your body, through your hands, to the object you are holding.

Some singers can't get through a performance without clutching something. I've seen their knuckles turn white, but it works. It's like a pipeline, transferring tension from your instrument to your body, then through your hands to whatever you're holding. Waving a sword around works the same way.

The only thing you have to remember, is to squeeza the coconut, no squeeza the banana!

What you are doing now is generating too much pressure in your voice.

It sounds good, but you're working too hard. Back off a bit!

It happens to everyone. After an hour, more or less, of no great activity upon its part, your instrument will always revert back to its former state of, shall I say... somnolescent meditation?

You have to tune it in all over again. Otherwise, you'll be forced to drive it a lot harder than you would have to, or intend to.

Baritone

I know this voice teacher that advocates bringing everything up from the bottom.

Ah, yes, I call that the steam shovel technique... using your arms to help you subconsciously open your throat, and perhaps even obtain the psychological sense of a lower placement. Yes, it does work, but only for the first five minutes or so of the lesson. After that, it tends to make the voice heavier and darker than it has any right to be.

Why bring up all the garbage in the lower part of your tessitura and try to stuff it into the upper part? It serves no purpose whatsoever in keeping the throat open or relaxed in the upper part of your tessitura. You're just carrying dead weight around!

There's another reason not to do anything to artificially add weight or color to the upper part of your voice. In doing so, that overblown sound is going to destroy your vowel and sweep away your consonant leaving you not only unintelligible but so vocally unwieldy that any concern for the emotional impact of the words, the drama, the music and even the notes involved, will be impossible to project.

Yes, I know you know what you're doing. You have an instinctive sense of what you're doing whether 'tis right or wrong. However, there's nothing you can do to fix anything that's already been done.

All you can do is fix something that's going to happen!

So, damn the torpedoes, full speed ahead, give it your best shot and don't apologize for anything!

Baritone

I think my EE vowel is getting more forward.

Well, your voice doesn't really want to accommodate an EE or AY vowel so any progress on the EE vowel only means that your instrument no longer shuts itself down like a clam and refuses to budge on it.

Bari.

Both guys I had studied with previously were baritones and they believed in "covering" the EE vowel. My EE never got any better.

In your voice, how the hell could it? Your voice was tight enough to begin with and to even try to distort it in such a manner will only make it more obstinate.

There's no way in hell you can free up any vowel by covering it.

What you're doing is imposing an abnormal mental and physical burden on your larynx. In the short run covering does work to a limited degree, but in the long run it kills off your high notes.

Bari.

It really destroys the voice. I've known a lot of singers, especially the lower voices...

Yeah! And they all get hung up on F's and F sharps!

Bari.

That's what my first teacher told me. The F sharp for baritone is the hardest note to sing because you're transitioning between registers... but I didn't have any high notes anyhow!

We'll just keep trying to free up your instrument the way we've been doing. Your E flat is beginning to show signs of life!

———

Whoa, you're no blackbird sitting in a tree watching all the girls go by.

I want you to move your whole body, not just your head.

I want you to face head on to whatever commands your attention.

If you have to lead with your shoulders... fine.

No head swiveling allowed!

An Ay vowel is an Ay vowel... it is not an Eh vowel.

Because your Ay vowel isn't strong enough to assert itself properly in the upper part of your tessitura, that's all the more reason why you have to make certain you are at least able to maintain its purity in the lower part of your voice.

Rigoletto was not born in Boston. I want E Quel Che Spegne... not Eh quehl cheh spehngeh. The purer the vowels, the stronger and clearer the message becomes.

What you must say is Ay, qwayl, kay, spay, nyay. It's nothing more than a pure Ay vowel interrupted by a series of consonants.

But you must remember to renew the Ay vowel any time a consonant precedes it, so you must also give me five Ay vowels.

When you finally get this pattern right, these four words will bond together and you can then begin to make some sense out of them... that's interpretation!

Fine... if you hadn't listened so hard to yourself, your tongue wouldn't have come up on the G. Your tongue came up, humped itself, and wonder of wonders... did not interfere.

You are still reaching for the pitch on the F sharps and G's.

When you think this way, your tongue goes along for the ride.

Bari.

I've been feeling like my nasal resonance is opening up a little bit, I'm beginning to feel more vibrations in there.

Well, your instrument is just starting to shake off a lot of its inherent tensions, loosening up a bit. Your voice is getting stronger, more resonant, so your placement will naturally improve also.

I'm not too sure whether your nasal resonance is really contributing to anything at all, but at least you have the awareness of what is needed, so if you feel it's working for you... great!

Tenor

They don't allow you to move on stage during an audition, that's the first thing they take away from you, I have to stay in one place.

Well, I can understand that, but you're giving me the impression I'm listening to a stick of wood!

Doing justice to the aria is not enough; you have to do more than just give them the impression you're alive and breathing.

They won't grumble if you take a step sideways, or backward, or better still, forward… they just don't want you to run amok!

With both feet in place, you can still twist your body in any direction you want to. You also have the option of reaching for the stars, begging for alms, fending off an adversary, and if you feel it to be relevant… scratch!

Don't do anything half-hearted; whatever movement or motion you make… you make it a strong one!

As long as you feel you are in character, do whatever you want.

═══════════════

Everything was fine until you closed down your nasal resonance. Your EE vowel needs all the help it can get. You must keep your sniffer open! I know it isn't easy, but your EE vowel's survival absolutely depends upon your nasal passages, the membranes, the two flaps inside your nose. You must become consciously aware of this.

Anytime you see someone deliberately grimacing, or showing their front teeth, even looking a little cross-eyed on their "high notes," that's what they are trying to do, they don't know any better.

The better your AY vowel gets, the more it influences your EE vowel to do the right thing. Since your EE vowel has this tendency to shut itself down under pressure, we're going to change Vino to Vayno.

I want you to say Finche Del Vayno. When your EE vowel decides to become a little more cooperative on the E's and F's in this aria, we can always change back.

I don't know if a person with a smaller tongue might have less trouble with it than some one with a larger one, but if every one had the tongue of a serpent and not that big ungainly muscle we all have to work with, I imagine everything would be a lot easier.

Your voice only gets "tight" when your tongue gets tired of being manipulated in the wrong way. Since your tongue gets involved in everything you do whether it wants to or not, it must be taught to react in a positive way.

It needs an absolute sense of purpose in what it's going to do.

The tongue must be trained to observe all the rules involved in the articulative process. You have to instill in it a reflex action to automatically assume any position you want it to.

Whether your tongue understands what it's doing or why, makes no difference. It's the same as training your dog or cat.

I feel that any teacher that neglects this portion of the vocal training process... couldn't teach a dog how to bark!

Now this time "Immenso Ptah" was a lot easier for you... you stayed in the same place. You didn't go up for the pitch... you went out for it, and you didn't open your mouth any more than you had to.

But it's a matter of trust... you're still making sure... so that's why you're working harder than you have to. All singers do, they can't help it... it goes with the territory.

Now for the last year or so we've been trying to discipline your larynx...

to indoctrinate it to accept commands... through the physical and the mechanical means we've employed... that's technique.

Then there's the mental aspect... where you combine the words and the music you have memorized, to convey the message you wish to deliver.

Now, the "Su Del Nido" you just sang came alive. It had spontaneity. That's because you believed in what you were saying... it not only made sense to you... but you meant it!

That's the only way to evoke the emotions involved; that's the spirit or the force that gives life to what you have to communicate.

You're telling me that your name is John Wellington Wells and that you're a dealer in magic and spells. That may well be, but I'm not going to believe anything you tell me!

When you came on stage, you not only cringed, but that prop you're clutching has more stage presence than you do!

Imagine for a moment that a six-hundred-pound gorilla has just entered the theater and is looking around for a seat. All he has to do is saunter over to wherever he may feel like sitting, pause a moment, and that seat becomes instantaneously available!

Now that's power!

If he held up a banana and informed the management that that was his ticket, no one would dare give him an argument.

Now, if you were a six-hundred-pound gorilla, and you told me your name was John Wellington Wells… I wouldn't dare doubt you!

Convince me.

=====

Many years ago a musicologist taught me that the tenor voice could not really sustain a pure EE vowel on or above a B natural.

He inferred that the vowel must, by natural laws, assume an AY vowel configuration or quality. If this did not occur, the tenor's instrument would either go into falsetto or crack.

I presume this natural law must also apply in some way to the baritone voice because your pure EE vowel has always seemed to want to self-destruct in the upper part of your tessitura, especially on your G's and A flats.

Now the good news. I believe this to be the first time your tongue has not come up, humped itself, or risen with the pitch on your F sharps and Gs on the EE vowel.

Your instrument has now reached the point wherein it seems to have blended the EE vowel sound with the AY vowel configuration in the uppermost part of your tessitura.

From here on in, even if your voice does get balky or a little obstinate under pressure, it won't close down on you. I think you're finally out of the woods.

You sound a little stilted in your Mio Figlio… you're not wrong but I want you to put a Y between your MEE and your OH vowel.

When you say MEE-YOH instead of MEE-OH it sounds a lot smoother, and feels freer. The same thing goes for Dio. DEE-OH is spoken as DEE-YOH. No one hearing you can tell the difference.

Almost any transition from the EE to OH vowel will work in this manner.

Now, I ask you, how can any one, in this day and age, make a recording and still sound flat or sharp or fuzzy or schmeary?

It happens all the time! When a tenor has to have twenty two intercuts to put across his version of an aria, I begin to wonder…

Nobody's in absolute tip-top shape all the time. When I sense some singer's voice beginning to betray him, I forgive him his transgressions. If it happens all the time… well, you can draw your own conclusions.

There's always going to be a void out there as far as perfection is concerned. Singers are far more sensitive to their own needs and imperfections than they are to anything else.

Well, it's only a G flat, but your resonance, your timbre, has a funny kind of a color on the G flat. It has a different quality to it.

It's not in any way a coarser or harder sound, it's something along the order of mahogany, mahogany, mahogany… chestnut! You understand what I'm saying?

Bari.

My voice is opening up some more?

I think so. Your voice is open and forward enough, and it's all in the same place, but there's a subtle kind of resonance change occurring, that I can't quite pin down. My guess would be that it's softening itself. In a sense, it's a by-product of everything we've been working for, so all I can tell you is this; what ever's taking place… is going to be to your advantage.

Your voice, being a law unto itself, has not the slightest interest in whether it be a coloratura soprano or a basso profundo.

Of course, you and I both know you weren't given a choice… you work with what you got. Now, every voice does indeed have its own set of unique or differing characteristics, but, this in no way will determine how it will be taught. I don't make any distinctions.

Any vocal teacher that adheres to any iron-bound method or cultivation process that will impose upon his students that one certain sound or quality of "tone" that he wants them to produce, will rob, you, the student, of your identity. All of his students will sound like carbon copies of each other.

They've been squeezed into a mold!

The end result is usually a quality of vocal "tone" that has no emotions of its own. Sure it's there… but who cares? You won't have a happy sound, a vibrant sound, a sound that proclaims to one and all…" born free".

———

Close, but no cigar. You're still dwelling on the L. Your T, D, and N consonants are much easier to spot when you are not quite correct, but your L consonant somehow manages to sound good even when it's wrong. That's damn near par for the course with all beginning vocal students… if a consonant's good enough to be understood… we tend to ignore the technique that produces it.

That's why voice teachers have their students go la la la on all their scales.

I know it feels right, but the tip of your tongue is still lingering too long on your upper front teeth.

You must learn to correct this; otherwise, when you have to sing L's in the upper part of your tessitura, you will make your voice work harder than it has to.

———

Hold on. Vocally you're in good shape, but from the interpretive viewpoint; Rigoletto's pain and anguish doesn't come across." Tu tace" was very well done, but your "Ahime" doesn't sound very woeful.

I don't want you to sing Ahime. I want inflamed ORATORY.

You have to make this word mean something more than…" What the hell you got in my soup here? Looks like a fly!"

Even though the Count Di Luna may be meditating, the opera house audience is eavesdropping on his thoughts. Whether he likes it or not, he has no choice... he has to share it with them!

Therefore, thou shalt not articulate, enunciate, or pronounce anything you must communicate to the audience to the stage, the scenery or the ceiling.

Now, when you say "Leonora e mia", her name has to conjure up all the passion you can muster. To give the words their full emotional value you must give each vowel ITS full value.

Technically, in order to know what you're dealing with, you have to reduce the words to their basic components.

They are not to be sung as Leh, Ow, Nor, Ah... Meh, Ah.

I want Lay, Yo, No-o-rAwe... Ay, Mee, Yaw.

I don't want you spreading your vowels any more than you're forced to.

(We'll now run Leonora up and down the flagpole! Ready?)

As well as you may have sung this aria, it isn't enough. Vocally you are damned good, almost authoritative, but... you're losing your stage presence... call it charisma! You don't quite know what to do with your body. You're too vague...

Nowadays, it almost seems to be a rule of thumb to cast a "singing actor" in certain roles. He's got the gut instinct and the presence of mind to assume the role and to make it believable.

But vocally, the audience gets cheated... they don't know any better. Many years ago I saw a performance of Jerome Kern's Showboat.

Everybody stunk! But when the black baritone sang "Old Man River," the house exploded... this guy could sing! He filled the whole theatre. No stage microphones for him.

Well, you sure as hell will never need a microphone, but from now on, we'll be working on whatever bodily movements seem to be the most natural to you ... and try to harness them somewhat.

In any kind of hostile confrontation you have to bluff or try to intimidate your adversary. What you just did was all very nice, but you sound like you're delivering a lecture on political correctness!

You're not giving me the impression of the turmoil involved… the hatred, envy, and malice…you're not menacing enough.

You want menace! I'll give you menace. All I have to do is to put my hand out… look you in the eye… and in no uncertain terms you will understand immediately what I'm after!

"Gimme a Quarter!!!…"

This is as good a way as any… to conjure up malevolance.

So put your paw out there… and we'll see what happens….

———

Well, I must admit, in some ways… you're beginning to make progress. You're almost starting to look good on stage. For what it's worth… consider this a compliment… you no longer look like you're going to throw up on the audience.

———

You're working your instrument overtime. All your La, La, La's sound good, but since your voice hasn't enough stamina to get through this aria, you must learn not to move your mouth every time you want to articulate an L.

You waste too much.

All you want is the "AWE" vowel preceded by the consonant L, and the only thing that moves is the tip of your tongue.

I know you're trying to convey a sense of purpose to these scales but don't make such a big deal out of them.

"Largo al Factotum" is really a tongue-in-cheek recitativo.

I don't want you to "sing" it… don't make it any harder for yourself than it has to be.

Just talk to me!

Vocally, your "Pari siamo" is going to need a helluva lot more going for it than good intentions. Just because you believe what you have to offer is viable, that's not good enough! You have to sell what you've got.

Even Moses had to peddle the Ten Commandments!

Here, take this hat, that's part of your costume. I want you to sell this hat to the audience. This hat is Pari Siamo! You're telling the audience to look it over, feel the material, notice the craftsmanship, how fortunate they would be to have one... to make you an offer you could not refuse!

No salesman ever really sells a product... he sells himself!

Singers are no exception... they also sell. More often than not, I have applauded someone with a flawed instrument... only because he made a believer out of me.

You not only have to believe in what you're selling, you have to project your persona, your aura, your own brand of individuality across the footlights...

otherwise... you'll fade into the scenery.

―――――――

Now that was good... all of a sudden your voice took on a quality you didn't have when we first started. I believed you when you said "Pieta, Pieta"... and I guess you also believed in what you were trying to say, so your voice took on an added dimension.

Now this is where the emotional aspect of your voice comes into play and overrides the mechanical and the mental homework we've been doing so far.

The more the words mean to you, the easier it all gets.

Just don't go bonkers!

―――――――

So you dropped your scepter, so what! Before you even opened your mouth, you retreated... you felt shamed.

No matter what happens, it isn't all that important! You can't ever allow some little mishap or other to get your nanny. Why give this prop any more importance than it deserves? You have to learn to improvise. Kick that stupid scepter across the stage like you meant to do it!

Can you imagine any conductor stopping a performance just because Rigoletto has to tie his shoelace?

Improvise!

You're on B naturals, you know that… right?

Bari.

Yeah!

Somebody would say you've solved the passagio problem. Con them a little. Just say something like… "gee, that's new to me… what's a passagio?" They'll probably respond with the obvious… "the passage between the registers!"

Now you've got 'em. "A passage between the registers…?"

"Now you've got me all confused. I've always understood my voice to have but one register. What do I need a passagio for?"

When all is said and done, you may, or may not have made them understand, that in addition to all your other vocal afflictions, why should you have had to endure the burden of a passagio?

─────────────

Well, it's taken almost four years for your instrument to achieve within itself the ease and freedom these other baritones were gifted with by Mother Nature. At this stage of the game, you're no better than they are, but… you at least know what the hell you're doing and why! You're learning how to survive.

Bari.

Yes. I've found that the better you get, the easier it is to get into bad habits, because you begin to believe in the fact that since you sound good… wherever you feel it, must be right also. I've heard of singers saying they feel it coming out the top of their head!

Yeah, and I wouldn't be surprised, if there's some one out there feeling and believing… his voice is coming out of his jock strap!

─────────────

Well, I must admit, your voice has now reached the point of no return.

You not only know how to get out of trouble, but even if your instrument does tighten up, you have more than enough left to carry you through.

You'll never have to endure the trials and tribulations of those legions of singers that are forced to rely primarily upon charm, intelligence, musicianship… and something in the heart… to survive.

You've added a voice.

Speaking of good people, we need
more like Filip Peterson…
if only Filip could bark.

"High" Notables

"High" Notables

"High" Notables

"High" Notables